MORE TECHNOLOGY FOR
THE REST OF US

MORE TECHNOLOGY FOR THE REST OF US

A Second Primer on Computing
for the Non-IT Librarian

NANCY COURTNEY, EDITOR

LIBRARIES UNLIMITED

AN IMPRINT OF ABC-CLIO, LLC
Santa Barbara, California • Denver, Colorado • Oxford, England

Library of Congress Cataloging-in-Publication Data
More technology for the rest of us : a second primer on computing for the non-IT
librarian / Nancy Courtney, editor.
    p. cm.
  Continuation of: Technology for the rest of us.
  Includes bibliographical references and index.
  ISBN 978-1-59158-939-6 (acid-free paper) — ISBN 978-1-59158-941-9
(ebook) 1. Libraries—Information technology. 2. Libraries—Technological
innovations. 3. Libraries and the Internet. 4. Digital libraries. 5. Digital
preservation. I. Courtney, Nancy. II. Technology for the rest of us.
  Z678.9.M66 2010
  025.00285—dc22   2009051166

ISBN: 978-1-59158-939-6
E-ISBN: 978-1-59158-941-9

14 13 12 11 10   1 2 3 4 5

This book is also available on the World Wide Web as an eBook.
Visit www.abc-clio.com for details.

Libraries Unlimited
An Imprint of ABC-CLIO, LLC

ABC-CLIO, LLC
130 Cremona Drive, P.O. Box 1911
Santa Barbara, California 93116-1911

This book is printed on acid-free paper ∞
Manufactured in the United States of America

CONTENTS

INTRODUCTION

This book is a continuation of *Technology for the Rest of Us: A Primer on Computer Technologies for the Low-Tech Librarian* (Libraries Unlimited, 2005). As with the earlier volume, the idea is to provide an introductory set of readings on technology topics that are fundamental to library operations today. The intended audience is librarians, library school students, or library staff members who are not in technology-related positions but who nevertheless want to have a greater understanding of the technologies that affect us on a daily basis. Each chapter author was chosen based on his or her expertise in a given topic and was asked to describe how the technology works and its current and potential uses for a nonspecialist audience. A variety of topics are covered, including web services, cloud computing, data preservation and curation, learning and content management systems, authentication, data visualization, open source software, and XSLT. A final chapter is not about a specific technology but explores effective communication between librarians and IT professionals. The hope is that the information given in this volume will help readers participate more fully in their libraries' discussions of information technology planning and policy.

Nancy Courtney

1

WEB SERVICES

Jason A. Clark

The web of the near-term future isn't about pages any more. It's about data, flying around, hopefully under the control of users, and offering a world of possibilities that few of us could have imagined just a few years ago.

—Marshall Kirkpatrick writing about web services on the blog ReadWriteWeb[1]

It is always interesting to read web industry observers like Kirkpatrick when they write about the future of the Web. Sometimes their thoughts can appear a bit off the cuff, but every once in a while something is written that captures the pulse of what is happening. When Kirkpatrick writes about data "flying around" instead of just HTML pages, he is recognizing the rise of web services. Over the last couple of years, as Web sites have evolved and become data providers, the nature of the Web has changed. One might even say that the Web has become a platform for developers, a means to share and exchange data for the purposes of creating new and exciting applications.

Web services is an umbrella term for a relatively simple concept: the ability to make requests to remote data sources and combine the data returned in response to the request into interesting new applications. *Mashup* and *remix* are terms frequently used to describe this action of combining data into something wholly new. Chances are you have seen, perhaps even used, web services before without even realizing it. The catch is that web services are a behind-the-scenes technology and commonly the domain of library systems folk. We will look to change this invisible technology into a transparent one by introducing the concept of web services and defining the key terms.

Next, we will take a look at examples of web services on the Web and in library settings. Then we will take a closer look at types of web services and walk through how to use one. Finally, we will talk about why web services matter and some resources for getting started and learning more.

WHAT IS IT? HOW DOES IT WORK?

Many of the technical definitions of web services focus on the protocols and languages that make up a web service without really touching on the simple meaning. In essence, web services are a technology for application integration allowing computers to communicate from machine to machine or program to program. They provide a standard of interoperability between disparate machines and systems because they are based on open standards like XML and HTTP. When we talk about web services, we are talking about three simple components:

1. The Web is used to deliver data from one computer to another computer. (HTTP)
2. The data that is passed between computers is structured according to certain rules or markup standards. (API, Structured Data)
3. Received data is transformed for display or used as instructions for additional data requests. (HTML or web scripting to produce HTML)

A *mashup*, our first key term, is a more specific term than web services. A mashup is a web application that uses or combines data from multiple sources into a single tool or user interface. Mashups rely on the above components of web services to function. A closer look at a library mashup scenario will provide some context. Imagine that you have just taken pictures of a recent library event and posted the pictures to your library's Flickr account. To make the images accessible, you could simply link to the Flickr account from your library home page, but what if you wanted the pictures to appear as a slide show on the home page itself? In this case, using web services and creating a mashup are viable options. Flickr, like many Web sites, allows people to make remote requests for the data that powers the Flickr site and even embed Flickr content into remote Web sites (see figure 1.1).

This action of providing access to data to be used in other contexts is the essence of a web service, and it is subject to a set of rules or allowed behaviors. When we talk of behavior and allowed actions, a second key term appears: *Application Programming Interface,* or *API.* An API is a way for developers to access parts of a web service provider and integrate its data with their own site. More specifically, an API prescribes a set of rules for access and coding requests to a remote computer that will return data according to these rules. In the Flickr example above, the API is the piece that allows the library Web site to request a list of images and related metadata from Flickr.

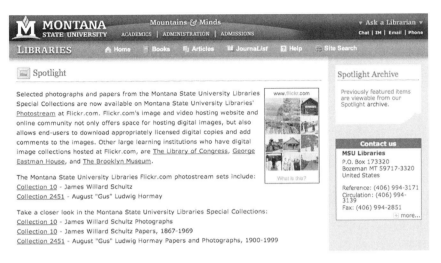

Figure 1.1. Example of Montana State University Libraries and Flickr Mashup. Code and explanation of the slide-show widget is available from the Flickr blog here: http://blog.flickr.net/en/2008/08/20/new-slideshow/.

Another essential piece of a web service is the need to have structured data returned so that the computer making the request can rely on data being in certain formats. *Structured data* is our third key term, and it is the glue that binds the mashup together. Structured data usually takes the form of XML (Extensible Markup Language) or JSON (Javascript Object Notation), which are lightweight markup languages that are easy to parse with a script and flexible enough to allow for communication between disparate systems. One can think of structured data as the encoded container for the useful pieces of data that will make the mashup work. These useful data snippets embedded within the structured data formats can include everything from weather forecasts to Amazon product sales lists to Google book cover thumbnail images. It all depends on the API you are requesting data from. In most cases, XML or JSON is the form of the structured data that is returned, but there are no hard and fast rules. In our Flickr widget example, the structured data that was returned was pure HTML in the form of an <object> tag that contained the full slide show.

Web Services and Mashups—Open Web Applications and Library Applications

The Flickr widget example above is a very simple demonstration of a web service and while useful, it doesn't really illustrate the power or potential of web services. The power and potential of web services are tied to Kirkpatrick's notion of data flowing freely, and more and more data is becoming accessible via web services seemingly everyday.[2] With this potential in mind, many sites on the Web and increasingly library Web sites and applications are starting to employ web services to enhance content. Twitter, the popular microblogging site, is just one example of a Web site that made its data available for developers and was rewarded with applications that at times eclipsed the functionality of the original Twitter web application. Examples along these lines include: twistori (http://twistori.com/), a data visualization of the emotions expressed by the Twitter community, and TweetDeck (http://tweetdeck.com/beta/), a desktop application for organizing and filtering Twitter. Facebook encourages users to create mini-applications that run within the Facebook environment and has made this service available through their Facebook Developers pages and an API (http://developers. facebook.com/). Amazon has made their full product listings available via a series of web services for years (http://aws.amazon.com/). Not to be outdone, Google has created web services for most of their applications and products (http://code.google.com/apis/). Of particular interest for libraries are the Google BookSearch API (http://code.google.com/apis/books/), which allows developers access to the digitized book collections within the Google Books program, and the ubiquitous Google Maps API (http://code. google.com/apis/maps/), which allows mapping and geolocation services for mashups and has produced many interesting map-based applications. A good example of the Google Maps API is "Where a Bill Becomes a Law" (http:// www.whereabill.org/), an educational and fun application that tracks the status of U.S. legislation, highlighting the actual locations where laws get made. Even traditional media outlets are embracing the potential of web services. The *New York Times* has released a series of APIs (http://developer.nytimes. com/docs) allowing developers to access current and historical data from movie reviews and best seller book data to news articles and even congressional voting records. Interesting mashups are emerging from the *New York Times* data APIs all the time. Take, for example, Reading Radar (http:// readingradar.com/), a web application that combines the *New York Times* Best Seller's API with Amazon's Product Listings API to provide pricing data, book ratings, book reviews and comments, and book cover thumbnails all integrated into a seamless and browsable interface (see figure 1.2).

As the possibilities for mashups continue to grow, more and more libraries are starting to use web services to supplement and improve services. Typically, libraries have been consumers of web services, and the list of mashups has been growing exponentially. It can be hard to earmark all of the recent work, but we will try to focus on some of the applications that are representative. The first group of library mashups involves supplements to the library catalog. Supplements and improvements to the catalog frequently take the form of book cover thumbnails, reviews, ratings, and tags/folksonomies. Two good examples in this area are the VuFind implementation of the catalog at George Mason University Libraries, which is using Amazon reviews to

Figure 1.2. Reading Radar mashup (http://readingradar.com/) showing *New York Times* and Amazon data working together.

ReadingRadar.com by John Herren.

give library users a voice about the catalog item (http://zoombox.gmu.edu/vufind/Record/419417/Reviews), and the VuFind instance at the Yale University Library, which is applying the Google Book Search API to allow for an electronic preview of content when it is available (http://yufind.library.yale.edu/yufind/Record/24516). The second group of library mashups is related to user interface redesign. These efforts have focused on reimagining the possibilities for browsing and searching library data. To this end, Texas A&M University Libraries has created a Yahoo maps interface (using the Yahoo Maps API) that allows a user to browse Geologic Atlas folios from around the United States by clicking on a map location marker (http://txspace.tamu.edu/handle/1969.1/2490) (see figure 1.3).

Similarly, Repository 66 uses the Google Maps API to provide a geographic interface to a list of library repositories worldwide (http://maps.repository66.org/). A third group of library mashups brings rich media into their applications or follows the widget model and enables library content to be embedded and used in new environments where their users are. On the media mashup end, Montana State University Libraries is using the blip.tv video API to create a browsable and searchable digital library collection of

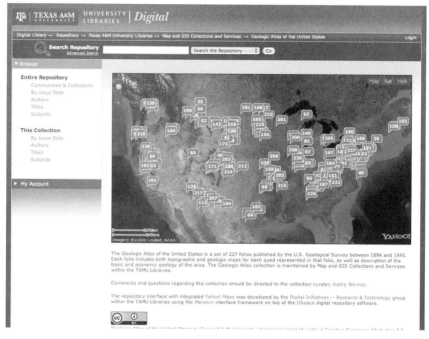

Figure 1.3. New modes of browsing and searching are realized in this Yahoo Maps API mashup with Texas A&M's University Library Geologic Atlas (http://txspace. tamu.edu/handle/1969.1/2490).

Geologic Atlas of the United States Digital Collection created by the Texas A&M University Libraries, Katherine H. Weimer, Curator.

nature and science videos created by elementary school students with its TERRApod project (http://www.terrapodcast.com/). On the widget end of things, OCLC is applying the WorldCat Search API to allow the creation of a WorldCat keyword search widget that can be embedded in blogs, iGoogle, or library Web sites (http://www.worldcat.org/blogs/archives/2009/03/ worldcat-keyword-search-widget.htm).

To a lesser extent, some library entities are providing web services and access to the data sets that power library applications. The leader in the library field has been OCLC. Last year, OCLC introduced "Grid Services" (http:// www.oclc.org/us/en/services/brochures/213093usf_worldcat_grid_ services.pdf), a set of APIs that allows access to various pieces of OCLC data. There has been some developer interest and new apps are emerging from the WorldCat Grid platform, but it is an area that is just starting to realize its potential. (A list of sample WorldCat Search API mashups is available at http:// www.worldcat.org/devnet/wiki/SearchAPIDemos.) Other entities to watch as library web service providers include the LibraryThing API (http://www. librarything.com/api) and the Talis semantic web platform (http://n2.talis. com/wiki/Main_Page).

TYPES OF WEB SERVICES

At this point, the patterns of a web service should start to become clearer, even familiar. A web services consumer makes a request for some data; a response is returned from a remote source or web services provider; and finally the response is parsed, displayed, or acted upon by the web services consumer. Yet, within this routine, there are different types or means of transmitting the messages between web service consumers and web service providers.

Currently, there are three primary types of web services. The first type is SOAP, which previously stood for Simple Object Access Protocol, but the acronym has now been dropped and SOAP is understood as a single word. The SOAP protocol is maintained by the W3C and available at the W3C website (www.w3.org/TR/soap). Fundamentally, SOAP is a protocol for transmitting messages, and those messages are formulated in XML. In practical terms, SOAP specifies how to construct the XML document that represents the message carrying the request and response. An example of a SOAP request is below.

```
<soapenv:Envelope

xmlns:soapenv="http://schemas.xmlsoap.org/soap/envelope/"

xmlns:xsd="http://www.w3.org/2001/XMLSchema"

xmlns:xsi="http://www.w3.org/2001/XMLSchema-instance">

<soapenv:Body>

<req:echo xmlns:req="http://localhost:8080/axis2/services/MyService/">

<req:category>classifieds</req:category>

</req:echo>

</soapenv:Body>

</soapenv:Envelope>
```

Unfortunately, there is really nothing simple about SOAP, and this complexity has led to a slow adoption and implementation rate. The rules that govern SOAP web services, while well-intentioned, have proven too complex and usually result in large XML documents that can slow down the simple data requests and responses needed to take advantage of the lean network transport protocol, HTTP, that powers the World Wide Web.

The second type of web service is XML-RPC, which stands for XML Remote Procedure Call. XML-RPC is one of the oldest types of web services, and it is still used frequently. The "pinging" services that let search engines know of page updates and blog update services that notify feed readers of new blog posts are XML-RPC web services. An example of an XML-RPC request might look like:

```
<?xml version="1.0"?>

<methodCall>
```

```
<methodName>examples.getResourceUpdate</methodName>

<params>

<param>

<value><i4>200</i4></value>

</param>

</params>

</methodCall>
```

In this case, the value of "200" would signify new content and the web service would carry out additional actions of harvesting the new content. XML-RPC is a very simple protocol and does not carry much information within the XML. This makes it a fast-messaging web service, but it limits the amount of data that can be transmitted. It works well for simple binary, yes-and-no-type actions, but XML-RPC's limitations have left developers looking for a web service type that can carry additional data nodes.

The third and final type of web service is REST, which stands for Representational State Transfer. REST is one of the most popular types of web services due to its simplicity and resemblance to a commonplace web activity—the act of submitting a URL. In fact, all of the examples of web services that we have discussed are REST-based web services. A typical REST request is below.

http://www.blip.tv/posts/?user=terrapoduser&pagelen=10&file_type=flv&skin=rss

Within the REST model, a web service consumer sends a service request to a web service provider as a URL with a set of parameters, and then the service response is returned as an XML data stream or another structured data format like JSON. It is up to the service consumer to parse the structured data stream and make use of the results. Due to their similarity to the URL request and highly optimized nature, REST-based services are the most common type of web service.

USING A WEB SERVICE: ANATOMY OF A REST REQUEST AND RESPONSE

Due to the ubiquity of the REST-based web services, it is likely that if you should choose to work with web services as a consumer, you will work within the REST method. Therefore, a closer look at an API employing the REST method will help to illustrate how all the web services components fit together and prepare you for your first steps toward using a web service to create a mashup. In this section, we will look at the common programmatic tasks that are shared across all programming languages for implementing a REST API request. The tasks we will follow are listed below.

1. Create a request object.

2. Add parameters and their values to the request.

3. Send the request.

4. Parse, display, or act upon the response.

In order to demonstrate how these tasks work in an actual web services set-ting, we are going to work through how to use the blip.tv REST API to make a simple video mashup. The blip.tv API allows for multiple REST methods centered around the main functions available in the native interface for the site—searching, getting metadata about videos, uploading videos, managing accounts, and so forth. Full documentation is available at http://blip.tv/about/api/. To make the blip.tv API work, a query is sent in the form of a URL, and blip.tv sends back XML or some other structured data format which is the raw material for our mashup. To see how this works, try to access the URL http://www.blip.tv/posts/?user=terrapoduser&pagelen=20&file_type=flv&skin=rss in your favorite web browser. A list of the most recently uploaded videos on the blip.tv instance of TERRApod is returned. The raw XML response to this method (which you can view in the source code of the resulting page) contains detailed information on these videos, and might look something like the XML in the image below (see figure 1.4).

If you are following along, you can see that we have worked through the first two web services tasks associated with the REST programming tech-nique. First, we have created a request object by deciding to ask for our most

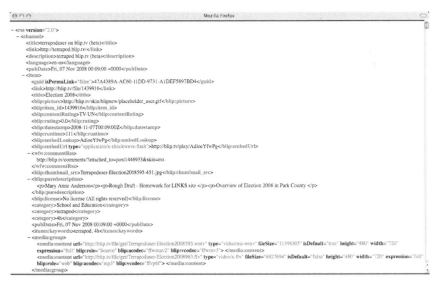

Figure 1.4. Example XML Response from blip.tv API.

recently uploaded blip.tv videos for the user named "terrapoduser" by submitting the base URL of *http://www.blip.tv/posts/?user=terrapoduser*. Second, we have added additional values and parameters to the request by appending the query string of *&pagelen=20&file_type=flv&skin=rss*. Each of these values specifies forms and quantities of data to return. "Pagelen" specifies the number of videos to return. "File_type" specifies flash video as the format to return and "skin" tells the XML format to return, in this case, RSS. Each of these parameters is explained in detail within the blip.tv API documentation. At any rate, we are ready to move into tasks three and four to finish the mashup.

When we send the URL request in full—http://www.blip.tv/posts/?user=terrapoduser&pagelen=20&file_type=flv&skin=rss—we are completing task three. After sending the request, we can expect a structured data response from the blip.tv API and we want to use the XML that is returned to build a show player for each of the videos and metadata returned. We got a glimpse of the metadata in figure 1.4 above. The final task involves transforming the metadata encoded in the XML returned into a format that a web browser can display. In this case, we use a PHP web script to traverse and cherry-pick the useful data from the XML result and reconstitute the data into a video-show player with some HTML that any web browser can display (see figure 1.5).

In this case, we rely on collecting the metadata and file information from each blip.tv video structured data container to enable the mashup. The most important piece of data in this case is the XML element <blip:embedLookup>, which holds a unique value that can be passed to the blip.tv Flash video player

Figure 1.5. Blip.tv video show player on TERRApod.

(an example is in bold below). The TERRApod player code is just simple HTML:

```
<p><strong>The Green Alien</strong></p>

<object type="application/x-shockwave-flash" classid="clsid:D27CDB6E-
AE6D-11cf-96B8–444553540000" height="390" width="640">

<param name="movie" value="http://blip.tv/play/AdXyQ4fwPg">

<param name="allowScriptAccess" value="always">

<param name="allowFullScreen" value="true">

<embed type="application/x-shockwave-flash" src="http://blip.tv/
play/AdXyQ4fwPg" allowscriptaccess="always" allowfullscreen="true"
height="390" width="640">

</object>

<p>01:52 (mins) | Produced by: Thomson, Ethan and Fry, Bryn Fry, and Barre,
Manon | <a class="download" href="http://blip.tv/file/get/Terrapoduser-
TheGreenAlien232.mov" title="Download: The Green Alien">Download</a>
</p>
```

The markup above is common html: <p> paragraph tags, a few <object> tags, and the <embed> tag. We needed some markup to place title, duration, and creator metadata. However, the most important piece is finding a method to bring the blip.tv Flash player along with its full-screen capabilities and sharing options into the TERRApod site. Being able to use these built-in functions and getting the unique media id (<blip:embedLookup> passed in dynamically with PHP) from the TERRApod local database to make the player run a specific video save a tremendous amount of time as we don't have to create a Flash video player from scratch. By leveraging the services and data that are part of the blip.tv API, MSU Libraries was able to create a video and podcasting Web site that could scale to larger capacities even with a developer team of one. To get a sense of the full TERRApod mashup, visit terrapodcast.com.

WHY DO WEB SERVICES MATTER?

"If, in the future, libraries want to be isolated islands in the ocean of content and information, they can ignore web services. But because much of what libraries do centers on providing information to library clientele and because information is increasingly more electronic—which causes libraries to overlap with many other organizations in the information sphere—it is necessary for libraries to cooperate and interact with a broad set of other organizations and their technical infrastructures. Web services provide mechanisms that allow libraries to expand their services in many important ways" (Breeding 2006).

As Breeding implicitly notes, libraries are increasingly looking for ways to participate in the general ecosystem of the Web. Web services with their reliance on open web standards like XML and HTTP offer the means for libraries to become integral data streams and sources for web applications. The reasons that web services matter are broad and varied. Among the highlights:

- Web services bring together disparate data sources.
- Web services can enhance existing sources of data.
- Web services improve usability and user interfaces.
- Web services enable access to content/data stores you could not otherwise provide (zip codes, news, pictures, reviews, etc.).
- Web services give small developer teams the ability to create large-scale web applications.
- Web services can enhance a site with a service that is not feasible for you to provide (maps, search, products, etc.).
- Web services provide an interoperable platform for library data.

In the short time since the rise of mainstream web services, the technology of web services has moved from merely something to be familiar with to something libraries and librarians need to participate in. The ubiquity of web services and the added functionality and data that many of the services provide can only improve modern library services.

GETTING STARTED

As has been mentioned numerous times in the chapter, creating a mashup or using a web service is just a series of simple actions: make a request; get a response in some form of structured data; parse the structured data for useful pieces; and, finally, display that data as HTML. If you are willing to study the API documentation and work through a little trial and error, you can make the move to mashup. The tips table below can help guide your thoughts as you consider getting started with web services.

Table 1.1. Web services tips

Tips—Getting started with web services
• Play in the sandbox—pick a service, study it.
• Yahoo Developer Central: http://developer.yahoo.com/
• Amazon Web Services Developer Connection: http://developer.amazonwebservices.com/connect/
• Google Code: http://code.google.com/

(*Continued*)

Table 1.1. Web services tips (*Continued*)

Tips—Consuming web services

- Pick a language or parsing tool.
- Find a few data sources (APIs) worth learning about.
- Make some requests and look at code in your browser.
- Think about added value, more efficient workflows.
- Browse around—many language libraries are already written.

Tips—Building web services

- URIs are your friends—that's your interface.
- Use simple CRUD (Create, Read, Update, Delete) functions over HTTP (Get, Delete, Put, Post).
- Keep verbs in API protocol intuitive and memorable.
- Start small—simple, read-only requests.
- Roll it out, beta version—once it's public you are restricted.

Tips—Web services data sources

- AllCDCovers.com http://www.allcdcovers.com/api
- ISBNdb.com http://isbndb.com/docs/api/index.html
- OpenDOAR http://www.opendoar.org/tools/api.html
- arXiv.org http://export.arxiv.org/api_help/
- Google Book Search APIs http://code.google.com/apis/books/
- LibraryThing APIs http://www.librarything.com/services/
- WorldCat Search API http://worldcat.org/devnet/wiki/SearchAPIDetails
* See programmableweb.

http://www.programmableweb.com/apis/directory

NOTES

1. Kirkpatrick's comment appears in the post titled "APIs and Developer Platforms: A Discussion on the Pros and Cons," published on March 3, 2008, and available at http://www.readwriteweb.com/archives/apis_platforms_pros_and_cons.php.

2. Programmable Web (http://www.programmableweb.com/) is a Web site that monitors the growth of web services daily. The mashup examples mentioned above were culled from the site. The catalog of web services represented there is impressive and if you want to keep up-to-date on the field as it exists on the open web, Programmable Web is your best resource.

REFERENCES

Breeding, Marshall. "Web Services and the Service-Oriented Architecture." *Library Technology Reports* 42, no. 3 (2006). http://alatechsource.metapress.com/content/n00527233756/.

ADDITIONAL READINGS

Engard, Nicole, ed. *Library Mashups: Exploring New Ways to Deliver Library Data.* Medford, NJ: Information Today, 2009.

Gardner, T. "An Introduction to Web Services." *Ariadne* 29, October 2, 2001. http://www.ariadne.ac.uk/issue29/gardner/intro.html.

Wusteman, Judith. "Realizing the Potential of Web Services." *OCLC Systems & Services: International Digital Library Perspectives* 22, no. 1 (2006): 5–9, doi: http://dx.doi.org/10.1108/10650750610640739.

2

DIGITAL DATA PRESERVATION AND CURATION

H. Frank Cervone

Librarians have been addressing issues related to the curation of materials since the first libraries were established. Academic and many public libraries are most familiar with issues of data curation in relationship to governmental data, such as census information or geographic data files. However, as information resources increasingly move to digital forms of representation, libraries and information agencies are attempting to address new challenges related to preserving these resources. Unlike preservation of traditional resources such as books, where there is an established knowledge base upon which librarians can develop and sustain practice, we are still in the formative stage of developing policies and strategies for the long-term preservation of digital information and resources.

WHAT IS DIGITAL DATA PRESERVATION AND CURATION?

Digital data preservation and curation are interrelated but separate topics. Today, most would consider digital data preservation to be a subset of the curation process. This is because digital preservation has been primarily concerned with the technical and managerial aspects related to maintaining a resource after it has been created. In this sense, it more closely models the traditional conceptualization of the data curation process.

This is in contrast to digital data curation, which has been defined as "the activity of managing the use of data from its point of creation to ensure it is available for discovery and reuse in the future" (Digital Curation Centre 2005). As can be seen in this definition, unlike traditional types of curation, digital curation is thought of as a complete life cycle process rather than an activity performed after the item has been created. This simple definition does not, however, indicate the incredible complexity inherent in the process of managing digital data to ensure future reuse. Carlson (2006) succinctly summarized several of the inherent issues in managing digital data in that often the data is "lost in some research assistant's computer, the data are often irretrievable or an indecipherable string of digits" (3).

The traditional curation model has been strongly influenced and modeled on the scholarly data creation process. In this process, researchers typically collect, research, and analyze data. Based upon this, the researcher authors an article or book, which is then published and disseminated. The disseminated articles and books are selected for storage, archiving, and preservation at various institutions, which take actions to ensure that these acquired resources are made for the longest time period possible.

The digital curation model is also based on the scholarly data creation model. However, to maintain digital objects an organization must be proactive in addressing certain issues during the life cycle of the object that traditionally have not been concerns with traditional curation. This is because digital objects are more volatile than traditional materials. There are several reasons for this volatility. For instance, digital objects such as web pages are extremely volatile because the content of pages can change, the overall structure of the site where the object is located changes, and the links between objects can change, move, or disappear (Hedstrom 1997). Additionally, it is well know that the life span of digital storage media is generally far shorter than that of traditional materials such as books (Beagrie and Jones 2001).

The complexity of the digital data curation process is clearly demonstrated in the definitive model of the life cycle, the DCC Curation Lifecycle Model (Digital Curation Centre). In the model, digital data objects move though several stages of life including:

- *Conceptualization*—The data objects are conceived and planned.
- *Creation/receipt*—In this stage the objects and their associated metadata are created and received according to the procedures and policies of the maintaining organization.
- *Appraisal/selection*—Objects that have been received are evaluated and selected for preservation in light of the applicable policies and procedures.
- *Ingestion*—The selected objects are transferred to the maintaining organization's storage facility, most typically an archive or repository.
- *Preservation actions*—Curators perform activities to ensure the long-term preservation and retention of the authoritative nature of the object to ensure the object maintains its integrity, authenticity, and reliability.
- *Storage*—In this stage the object is physically stored in accordance with applicable standards to meet current and long-term needs; objects may be stored in multiple formats or in multiple places to ensure short-term and long-term needs are met.

- *Access, usage, and reusage*—Data is made available to designated users; access control and authentication may be applied to objects to limit use to specific purposes or audiences.
- *Transformation*—New objects are created from existing objects to support migration to newer object formats or support new uses of the objects in a differing context.

In addition to this life cycle process, objects occasionally enter other life-changing stages:

- *Disposal*—Data objects that have not been selected for long-term curation. In some cases, the data is transferred to a more appropriate maintenance organization while in other cases the data is destroyed in accordance with institutional policies or in response to legal requirements.
- *Reappraisal*—Data objects that fail routine validation procedures typically need to be reevaluated to determine whether continued long-term maintenance and curation is viable and desirable.
- *Migration*—Data objects occasionally need to be migrated to new formats in response to changes in hardware and software; failure to migrate the objects in these circumstances would either inhibit or prohibit continued long-term use.

STANDARDS IN DIGITAL CURATION AND PRESERVATION

Standards play a significant role in the overall preservation and curation of digital objects. There are standards related to repository architecture, object description, descriptive metadata, technical metadata, and discipline-specific metadata.

Perhaps the most important overall standard in this area is ISO (International Standards Organization) standard 14721—the OAIS (Open Archival Information System) Reference Model (CCSDS 2002). While the goal of the reference model is multipurpose, perhaps its most important role has been to define a framework for describing the architectural and operational characteristics of a digital repository.

The OAIS Reference Standard

The OAIS model is based upon a fairly simple environmental model that consists of three actors—producers, consumers, and management/administration. Producers are people or systems that create the objects to be preserved. Consumers are people or systems that interact with services provided by an OAIS-compliant repository to find and obtain objects of interest. Management is the intermediary role the maintainers of the repository play in establishing policies and procedures for obtaining and disseminating objects (see figure 2.1).

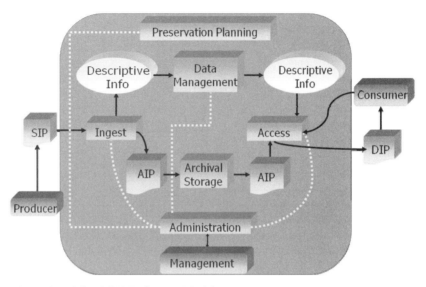

Figure 2.1. The OAIS Reference Model.

Perhaps the most important architectural concept in the model is that of *information package,* which is a logical construct that includes the object to be preserved (the content information) and preservation description information (known as the PDI) related to the object. Note that an information package can contain more than one content information object; for example, a journal article that contains both text and the image files that are interspersed throughout the text. The PDI typically consists of four types of preservation information:

- *Provenance*—Describes the origin of the content information, the chain of custody of the content source since its inception, and, in most cases, the history of the information including data related to any processing of the content that may have occurred.
- *Context*—Metadata that describes how the content information related to other objects outside the information package. For example, if the information package were an image from a chapter in a book, this metadata would describe how the image relates to the chapter. The metadata related to the chapter object would describe how the chapter related to the overall book.
- *Reference*—Provides identifying information that uniquely identified the content information. Standards-based examples might be an ISBN for a book, an ISSN for a journal, or a DOI for a journal article; however, reference can also be provided by providing a set of attributes that uniquely distinguish one instance of content information from another.
- *Fixity*—Provides a mechanism for identifying alteration of the content information. This could be provided by a cyclical redundancy check (CDC) or a check sum of the data in the information package.

As is demonstrated in the model, there are differences between information packages that are submitted to, preserved in, and disseminated from an OAIS-compliant repository. Variations in the packages at different stages in the life cycle are required for multiple reasons. For instance, content going into a repository may not have all the representation or preservation information needed to store the object successfully. An example of this might be a researcher submitting a TIFF file to a repository for long-term curation. During submission to the repository, the researcher may not know all the technical details about the image that would be required for the successful ingestion (storage) of the object, so a repository manager may have to intervene and create or generate the required metadata before the object can be successfully ingested. On the other side, another researcher may want to use that same TIFF file, but he may need to have it presented in JPG format rather than TIFF due to considerations in his computing environment.

As a result, there are three different types of information packages and these are referred to as submission information packages (SIP), archival information packages (AIP), and dissemination information packages (DIP). A SIP is a package that is sent to the repository by a producer. The format of the content and associated metadata of the SIP is defined locally at the repository level and made known to the producer. In general, a SIP will contain content information and some PDI, usually of a descriptive nature.

Within the repository, SIPs are transformed into AIPs for long-term storage. Every AIP has a comprehensive set of PDI for the coupled content information. The relationship of SIPs to AIPs is complex as multiple SIPs may be required to form an AIP. For example, multiple SIPs representing individual articles can be used to form a single AIP representing a journal issue. Alternatively, a single SIP may be transformed into multiple AIPs. A case where this might be used is when a JPG image SIP is accepted but stored in two different AIPs where one contains the original JPG format but the second contains a transformation of the JPG into TIFF format.

Information retrieved by a consumer from the repository is disseminated in a DIP that is constructed from one or more AIPs. Depending on the nature of the request, the DIP returned to the consumer may or may not have the complete PDI. In most cases, the packaging information that is returned to the consumer is based on the nature of the request and therefore can be in varying forms. In all cases, however, the packaging information returned provides enough information for the consumer to identify the object requested.

Metadata Standards for Digital Curation and Preservation

There are many different metadata schemes that are used in digital curation and preservation efforts and in this chapter we can only begin to touch upon some of the most important standards. Some of these metadata schemes are specifically developed to support curation and preservation (such as PREMIS), whereas others find applicability and use in a broader range of activities.

Built upon the OAIS Reference Model, PREMIS (Preservation Metadata: Implementation Strategies) is the foundation for metadata related to preservation. Representing a wide cross section of interests including libraries, museums, archives, and commercial interests, the PREMIS standard addresses issues related to creation, management, and usage of digital objects. PREMIS is not a metadata standard in itself but a data dictionary that provides a basis for implementing a preservation metadata scheme within a repository. The data dictionary defines metadata elements that "represent the information most preservation repositories need to know to preserve digital materials over the long-term" (PREMIS Editorial Committee 2008, p. 1).

METS (Metadata Encoding and Transmission Standard) is a structural metadata scheme commonly used in repositories as the basis for describing the composition and relations of content information in information packages. More formally, METS is "a data encoding and transmission specification, expressed in XML, that provides the means to convey the metadata necessary for both the management of digital objects within a repository and the exchange of such objects between repositories (or between repositories and their users)" (METS Editorial Board 2007, p. 5). Digital objects encoded in METS can be exchanged transparently among repositories and systems because METS provides the basis for creating structural metadata that describes the composition of an object and its relationship to other objects. Furthermore, when digital objects are shared, the data transfer syntax of METS provides a common syntax for implementing the exchange of objects among repositories and systems.

MODS is a descriptive metadata scheme frequently used in repositories to associate original description metadata elements with information packages. Based on natural language, MODS does not enforce strict adherence to the use of any particular cataloging code. Because of these characteristics, descriptive data in MODS can often be created more easily and quickly than it can be in other descriptive metadata schemes, such as the MARC 21 bibliographic format. When compared to the Dublin Core metadata scheme, MODS is a richer descriptive format because it is based on a fuller implementation of the MARC 21 fields. However, MODS only includes a subset of MARC fields, so descriptive data from MARC 21 records converted to MODS frequently will not reconvert to MARC format without loss of specificity in field tagging and sometimes without the complete loss of certain data fields that do not map between the two formats.

MIX (NISO standard Z39.87–2006) is an example of a specialized, technical metadata scheme. While METS is used to describe the structure of objects, the MIX metadata scheme provides metadata elements that describe the technical aspects of images that result from photography and scanning

(NISO 2006). For example, MIX provides metadata elements that describe the compression scheme and compression ratio used to create an image file as well as the image width, height, color space, and color profile of the image itself.

A plethora of metadata schemes have been developed for specific applications. The VERS metadata scheme evolved out of the electronic records strategy recommendations of the State of Victoria in Australia. The VERS metadata scheme provides structural and descriptive information related to the creation and maintenance, management, destruction, and transfer of electronic public records. The MPEG-7 metadata standard provides a standard syntax for describing multimedia content. Another example of a structural and descriptive metadata scheme, MPEG-7 provides both elements, which define the structure and relationships of the data streams that compose the multimedia content and additional descriptive elements that are designed to enable searching, filtering, and browsing of multimedia content streams. HDF is an emerging scheme for storing and using very large-scale data sets that cannot be managed within the constraints of traditional relational database systems.

SOFTWARE FOR DIGITAL CURATION AND PRESERVATION

In order to properly curate and preserve digital objects, *repository software* must be used to manage the objects. Repository software typically offers facilities for ingesting, categorizing, describing, storing, and disseminating objects. While not mandatory, ideally the software will conform to the OAIS reference model. While there are several commercial products available (CONTENTdm and DigiTool being the most commonly used), this area of software has been dominated by open source products such as EPrints, DSpace, and Fedora.

CONTENTdm

Originally developed at the University of Washington's Center for Information Systems Optimization and now marketed by OCLC, CONTENTdm is not repository software per se but rather digital collection management software. This distinction, while subtle, is important. CONTENTdm provides many services that make it appear to have the functionality of a repository; however, it does not provide full OAIS-based object management services. Instead, the model of CONTENTdm is most similar to a database management system that keeps track of the locations of digital files and the relationships between these files.

CONTENTdm can support compound data types, but the relationships within the object are not defined via a structural metadata scheme. Given the underlying architecture of CONTENTdm, only descriptive metadata schemes are associated with objects; everything else is controlled and defined as configuration options within the software. Because of this, many in the repository community do not consider CONTENTdm to be a suitable solution for digital object management. Nonetheless, the advantage CONTENTdm enjoys in comparison to other repository solutions is that it is simple to install and use, and provides an easy way to make digitized objects available to patrons. For libraries and other institutions that do not have the extensive resources or personnel available to implement a repository solution, CONTENTdm provides a low-barrier entry to the management of digital objects.

DigiTool and Rosetta

Originally, ExLibris developed the DigiTool product to serve as a complete repository solution. However, as the limitations of the end-to-end architecture in the original version of DigiTool became evident and acceptance of the OAIS model evolved, the company changed its strategy. Today, the model used by ExLibris is conceptually similar to that of Fedora where the digital asset management component is implemented as a distinct software product, not inherently tied to the presentation and administration interface. In the latest version of DigiTool, the product focuses on the management and presentation components of a digital repository and the backend object storage and preservation tasks have been moved to Rosetta. Having been developed later than most of the other repository products, Rosetta was designed from the beginning to be OAIS-compliant. Additionally, it is specifically designed to support a distributed architecture with separate permanent and working repositories. In addition to potential performance benefits, this distributed architecture begins to help address some of the issues related to scalability in support of extremely large data storage.

DSpace

DSpace is an open source repository package originally codeveloped at the Massachusetts Institute of Technology with support from Hewlett-Packard. DSpace is notable in that it was the first general-purpose repository software to gain a significant following. Easy to install and use "out of the box," DSpace is now installed at over 500 institutions worldwide.

The initial architecture of DSpace was an end-to-end solution, but the problems inherent in this model began to become apparent not long after DSpace started to gain widespread adoption. In 2007, development of DSpace was turned over to the DSpace Federation, which uses a community development model similar to that of the Apache (web server) Foundation. Because of this community-based model, a community of additional supporting software has begun to develop around the DSpace initiative. One example of this is that the alternative user interface developed at Texas A&M University, *Manakin* has been developed to address specific needs of DSpace community members.

DSpace is scheduled to undergo a major architectural revision and enhancement in the version 2.0 release. This, along with the merger of the DSpace Federation and Fedora Commons into a single entity to be known as the Duraspace Federation, promises to extend the vitality of the DSpace platform and community into the foreseeable future.

EPrints

Originally released in 2000, EPrints was developed and is maintained at the University of Southampton. As the first repository software package to be released, it is one of the most widely used repository software packages in the world, although its use in North America has been low. Originally developed as a method for managing pre- and post-print versions of traditional journal articles, one of the unique characteristics of the EPrints software is that it contains many features that are commonly found in document management systems.

Given this background, EPrints has been heavily focused on issues related to the preservation of text-based materials; however, the underlying repository structure is robust and OAIS-compliant. EPrints is one of the few repository packages that has successfully maintained an end-to-end solution architecture for repository management integrating a flexible user interface with long-term preservation tools. Having evolved significantly in its short life span, EPrint is uniquely positioned to address issues related to journal preservation in addition to being used as a generalized repository to provide services for a wide range of materials, including scientific data, multimedia, teaching materials, exhibitions, and performances.

FEDORA

FEDORA, originally developed at Cornell University and currently managed by the Fedora Commons organization, is a modular digital object management system upon which the components necessary for a digital repository can be developed. Architecturally, FEDORA has the most robust and flexible architecture of all current repository systems. The flexibility of the architecture makes it possible to represent any type of digital object within the repository framework. Because metadata and information content are treated uniformly in the architectural model, any appropriate metadata format can be applied to digital objects.

This flexible architecture has also been a drawback in some contexts. Unlike other repository software solutions, FEDORA is not a solution that is usable "out of the box." Installing and using FEDORA requires a high level of technical skill and sophistication. Furthermore, because the focus on development to date has been on the data store and its model, significant local customization must be done to the user interface to have a workable product.

Offsetting these drawbacks, the FEDORA user community has been quite active in developing solutions to various interests in the community. Examples of this include ISLANDORA, which is a module developed at the University of Prince Edward Island that allows Drupal content management system users to use Drupal as a front end to managing and viewing objects in a FEDORA repository, as well as Fez, a PHP and MySQL-based front end to FEDORA developed at the University of Queensland.

Zentity

The newest entry in repository software is Zentity. Available at no charge from Microsoft Research, this product is designed to provide tools and services to develop a digital repository quickly and easily. Designed specifically to address the needs of research output, the product includes a data model with predefined entities, such as lecture, publication, paper, presentation, and video with basic properties and relationships for each of these. Because it is a Microsoft product, unlike other repository software packages that often provide flexibility in selecting back-end support components, Zentity requires Microsoft SQL Server 2008 and .NET Framework version 3.5 on the back end. Support for various formats and services such as full-text search, OAI-PMH, RSS and Atom Syndication, BibTeX import and export, SWORD, AtomPub, RDFS, and OAI-ORE are included as part of the distribution (Microsoft 2009).

ISSUES IN DIGITAL CURATION AND PRESERVATION

Given the complexity and broad scope of digital curation and preservation efforts, it is not surprising to find a multitude of issues and concerns related to both topics. Some problems are specific to particular formats that are to be preserved or curated digitally, but most concerns apply in one way or another to all types of digital curation and preservation.

At the most basic level, digital curation efforts need to ensure that the same stream of bits originally stored remains stable over long periods of time. This is not a given as all types of physical media are susceptible to *bit rot,* an event that occurs when the bits of file in storage are inadvertently changed. Most often, this is caused by physical deterioration of the physical media; however, stray magnetic particles in the atmosphere have also been identified as a potential cause of this as well (O'Gorman et al. 1996).

Bit rot is the most elementary problem in ensuring that digital objects are not lost over the course of time. Bit rot can be prevented by ensuring copies of digital objects are housed in multiple data stores (Keeton et al. 2006), integrity checks are performed on a regular basis (Kapali and Donald 1975), and data on a physical medium is migrated to a newer media on a regular basis (Rosenthal et al. 2004).

As libraries increasingly store data from varied sources, a concern for the repository manager is how to ensure preserved data is usable in the future. Some types of digital objects, such as the PDF file format, are so ubiquitous that it is assumed a logical migration path from version to version of the format will be provided to ensure these objects can be used well into the future. Long-term usage of more specialized and niche file formats, such as those currently used to gather various types of scientific data, is not necessarily as secure.

Application software has a relatively short life span in the grand scheme of things. Often due to constraints in software design or due to intentional decisions to force obsolescence (and subsequent required migration), application software is not able to process file formats that are several generations old. Because of this, objects and data that have been preserved may not be usable in the future without extraordinary intervention to migrate the objects and data to a new and potentially different format. Even with migration, certain file formats will simply cease to exist as software falls out of use. WordStar word processing files are an example of this. A further complication is that older software may only run on certain hardware or operating system platforms. When these platforms cease to exist, a similar problem arises. In all of these cases, abandoned file formats will either have to be migrated to a completely new format (and possibly new application system) or repository managers will need to provide *emulators* that will allow old applications to continue to function and process these outdated formats in newer computing environments.

Another pressing concern is that as repositories and the objects within them become larger, traditional methods for managing data are breaking down. For example, in a very large repository that contains petabytes of information, the process of migrating data to avoid bit rot becomes impractical. In addition to the cost of such migrations, the process itself becomes overwhelming as it does not scale. Consequently, as repositories evolve, the methods used to manage those repositories will have to change radically in order to manage the massive amounts of data they will contain (Szalay 2008).

SOME GUIDELINES FOR DATA STEWARDSHIP

Data curation as a concept is still in its infancy. Throughout the history of information technology, long-term data retention and access have been issues, but typically these were concerns within specific contexts. In many cases, the major concern related to data retention focused on ensuring data was available to recover after a disastrous event. More recently, data retention has also focused on issues related to legal requirements compliance (Wrozek 2002).

Over the short period of time that data curation and stewardship have come to gain importance in the work of libraries, several guidelines and best practices have developed. Berman (2008) summarized these as general principles, and they can be adapted for digital library use as follows:

1. *Make a plan*—The organization must have a well-defined and communicated plan for curating and preserving its data, from creation to end of life; organizations must explicitly define what the end of life of a digital object is;

2. *Be aware of costs and include them in your overall budget*—All costs must be considered including one-time costs such as hardware, software, expert support, and time as well as ongoing costs of maintenance. In some cases, it may be more cost-effective to regenerate data rather than preserve it;

3. *Associate metadata with your data*—Metadata is the critical link that allows digital objects to be discovered; follow relevant standards to ensure that objects can be used in the long term;

4. *Make multiple copies of valuable data*—Any digital object worth preserving needs "insurance"; store digital objects in multiple datastores and ensure that at least one of those datastores is an off-site location;

5. *Plan for the transition of digital data to new storage media ahead of time*—Include the costs of migrations in every yearly budget plan; new storage and software technologies, file format migrations, and staff time must be considered on a yearly basis as migration is an ongoing process. Data must be migrated to new technologies before storage media becomes obsolete;

6. *Plan for transitions in data stewardship*—All organizations change and evolve over the course of time and software changes as well, so do not plan as if data objects will remain in the same repository in perpetuity;

7. *Determine the level of assurance required when choosing how to archive data*—Not all data objects are equally important nor do they all need to be retained for the same length of time; consider flexible retention and validation policies to address these differing needs;

8. *Tailor plans for preservation and access to the expected use*—The example Berman uses summarizes the issue perfectly: Gene-sequence data used daily by hundreds of thousands of researchers worldwide may need a different preservation and access infrastructure from, say, digital photos viewed occasionally by family members;

9. *Pay attention to security*—Ensure that the repository infrastructure can support what must be done to maintain the integrity and access policies of the digital objects; and

10. *Know what specific regulations you need to comply with*—Depending on the nature of your data objects, your repository may need to enforce policies related to copyright, HIPAA (the Health Insurance Portability and Accountability Act of 1996) compliance, federal agency publishing and reporting expectations, or any other number of policies and regulations; ensure that the data curation policies and procedures of your organization are compliant with these.

THE FUTURE OF DIGITAL CURATION

What the future holds for digital curation is anyone's guess. Clearly, we are at the beginning of a process that will evolve. Much of our current-day practice is based on what we know from past experience; however, as Rusbridge (2006) has pointed out, often our expectations of the future based on past experience are woefully incorrect. He points out that many common beliefs related to digital curation, such as the idea that digital preservation is very expensive or that file formats become obsolete very rapidly, do not necessarily stand up to test under scrutiny.

This theme of uncertainty is also reflected in the comments of Myers (2006):

> In planning for the next-generation of digital data curation and preservation capabilities, it is important to question our assumptions. While the expertise gained over centuries in curation and preservation will be central to robust solutions, it will be necessary to disentangle principles of information management from practices that actually represent compromise based on the current limits of technologies and organizational structures. Conversely, while technological progress will play a driving role, complex sociotechnical issues will be faced in defining practical solutions that align with cultural and economic realities and are "just complex enough" to serve society's needs. If the web analogy is broadly valid, we are about to enter a period of rapid progress, new ideas, and new partnerships that will dramatically change and improve our ability to understand the world's information. (p. 2)

So what should a library do about digital curation? A reasonable approach is to take a middle path. Pay attention to best practice and emerging trends; choose software that has a large base of users and an active development community; and adopt metadata schemes that are broadly used. But at the same time, do not become too tied to any one vendor or particular preservation ideology. As both Rusbridge and Myers imply, the world changes rapidly and we need to be flexible enough to change with it. There is a good chance that in 10 years, many of the concepts in this chapter will appear to be quaint, and we will sit around wondering why people did things that way or proffered that particular bit of advice. That's not a problem because if the landscape of digital curation and preservation did not change, we probably would not be doing a very good job.

REFERENCES

Beagrie, Neil, and Maggie Jones. *Preservation Management of Digital Materials.* Digital Preservation Coalition, 2001, http://www.dpconline.org/graphics/handbook/ (accessed on May 24, 2009).

Berman, Francine. "Got Data? A Guide to Data Preservation in the Information Age." *Communications of the ACM* 51, no. 12 (2008): 50–56, http://doi.acm.org/10.1145/1409360.1409376 (accessed on May 23, 2009).

Carlson, Scott. "Lost in a Sea of Science Data." *The Chronicle of Higher Education* 52, no. 42 (2006): A35, http://chronicle.com/free/v52/i42/42a03501. htm (accessed on April 30, 2009).

Consultative Committee for Space Data Systems (CCSDS). *Reference Model for an Open Archival Information System (OAIS).* Recommendation for Space Data System Standards: National Aeronautics and Space Administration, 2002, http://public. ccsds.org/publications/archive/650x0b1.pdf (accessed on May 21, 2009).

Digital Curation Centre. "Curation Lifecycle Model." n.d. http://www.dcc.ac.uk/ docs/publications/DCCLifecycle.pdf (accessed May 18, 2009).

Digital Curation Centre. "Frequently Asked Questions from Data Curators." May 31, 2005, http://www.dcc.ac.uk/FAQs/data-curator (accessed May 15, 2009).

Hedstrom, Margaret. "Digital Preservation: A Time Bomb for Digital Libraries." *Computers and the Humanities* 31, no. 3 (1997): 189–202, http://www.springerlink. com/index/H73V57H6587K4L7N.pdf (accessed on May 20, 2009).

Kapali, P. Eswaran, and D. Chamberlin Donald. "Functional Specifications of a Subsystem for Data Base Integrity." *Proceedings of the 1st International Conference on Very Large Data Bases.* Framingham, Massachusetts, 1975, http://doi.acm. org/10.1145/1282480.1282484 (accessed on May 3, 2009).

Keeton, Kimberly, Dirk Beyer, Ernesto Brau, Arif Merchant, Cipriano Santos, and Alex Zhang. "On the Road to Recovery: Restoring Data after Disasters." *ACM SIGOPS Operating Systems Review* 40, no. 4 (2006): 235–48, http:// doi.acm.org/10.1145/1218063.1217958 (accessed on May 13, 2009).

METS Editorial Board. *Metadata Encoding and Transmission Standard: Primer and Reference Manual.* Digital Library Federation, 2007, http://www.loc.gov/ standards/mets/METS%20Documentation%20final%20070930%20msw.pdf (accessed on May 16, 2009).

Microsoft. "Zentity V1.0." Microsoft, n.d. http://research.microsoft.com/en-us/ projects/zentity/ (accessed on May 27, 2009).

Myers, James D. "The Coming Metadata Deluge." *ARL/NSF Workshop on Long-Term Stewardship of Digital Data Collections.* 2006, http://www.arl.org/ bm~doc/metadata.pdf (accessed on May 15, 2009).

NISO. *Data Dictionary—Technical Metadata for Digital Still Images.* National Information Standards Organization, 2006, http://www.niso.org/kst/reports/ standards/kfile_download?id%3Austring%3Aiso-8859-1=Z39-87-2006. pdf&pt=RkGKiXzW643YeUaYUqZ1BFwDhIG4-24RJbcZBWg8uE4v WdpZsJDs4RjLz0t90_d5_ymGsj_IKVa86hjP37r_hExj8UR8r_jBdk_ZQaQ Io5DPbfamndQa6zkS6rLL3oIr (accessed on May 14, 2009).

O'Gorman, T. J., J. M. Ross, A. H. Taber, J. F. Ziegler, H. P. Muhlfeld, C. J. Montrose, H. W. Curtis, and J. L. Walsh. "Field Testing for Cosmic Ray Soft Errors in Semiconductor Memories." *IBM Journal of Research and Development* 40, no. 1 (1996): 41–50.

PREMIS Editorial Committee. *Premis Data Dictionary for Preservation Metadata.* 2nd ed. Library of Congress, 2008, http://www.loc.gov/standards/premis/ v2/premis-2-0.pdf (accessed on May 13, 2009).

Rosenthal, David S. H., Rema Roussopoulos, T. J. Giuli, Petros Maniatis, and Mary Baker. "Using Hard Disks for Digital Preservation." Berkeley, CA, 2004, http://berkeley.intel-research.net/maniatis/publications/hard-disk.pdf (accessed May 24, 2009).

Rusbridge, Chris. "Excuse Me ... Some Digital Preservation Fallacies?" *Ariadne*, no. 46 (2006), http://www.ariadne.ac.uk/issue46/rusbridge/ (accessed on April 30, 2009).

Szalay, Alexander S. "Scientific Publishing in the Era of Petabyte Data." *Proceedings of the 8th ACM/IEEE-CS Joint Conference on Digital libraries*. Pittsburgh, PA, 2008, http://doi.acm.org/10.1145/1378889.1378932 (accessed on May 23, 2009).

Wrozek, Brian. *Electronic Data Retention Policy*. SANS Institute, 2002. http://www.sans.org/reading_room/whitepapers/backup/electronic_data_retention_policy_514?show=514.php&cat=backup (accessed on May 27, 2009).

ADDITIONAL RESOURCES

An Audit Checklist for the Certification of Trusted Digital Repositories—http://www.rlg.org/en/pdfs/rlgnara-repositorieschecklist.pdf—An essential guide to criteria necessary to ensure a digital repository maintains and sustains content integrity. Originally produced for the Research Libraries Group, which was acquired by OCLC. Ironically, this document no longer appears to be available online.

Briefing Paper—the OAIS Reference Model—http://www.ukoln.ac.uk/projects/grand-challenge/papers/oaisBriefing.pdf—A good, comprehensive overview of the OAIS reference model, including a wide range of references to materials from various disciplines that might be deposited in a repository.

The Case for Institutional Repositories: A SPARC Position Paper—http://www.arl.org/bm~doc/instrepo.pdf. One of the seminal works in the area of digital preservation. Some of the references and issues have evolved since the report was written, but this is a foundational work for anyone interested in the issues related to institutional repositories. Written by Raym Crow for the Association of Research Libraries.

Digital Curation Centre—http://www.dcc.ac.uk/—One of the major centers for research into the issues related to digital-data preservation and curation.

METS metadata standard official Web site—http://www.loc.gov/standards/mets/.

MIX metadata standard official Web site—http://www.loc.gov/standards/mix/.

MODS metadata standard official Web site—http://www.loc.gov/standards/mods/.

MPEG-7 standard information—http://www.prov.vic.gov.au/vers/standard/spec_02/.

The Research Library's Role in Digital Repository Services—http://www.arl.org/bm~doc/repository-services-report.pdf—A comprehensive overview of the emerging and future role of academic and research libraries in managing digital preservation and curation services. A report produced by the Association of Research Libraries Digital Repository Issues Task Force.

Understanding PREMIS—http://www.loc.gov/standards/premis/understanding-premis.pdf—A general introduction to the metadata standard. Authored by Priscilla Caplan for the Library of Congress.

VERS metadata standard official Web site—http://www.prov.vic.gov.au/vers/standard/spec_02/.

3

CLOUD COMPUTING: DISTRIBUTED POWER, REMOTE STORAGE, AND WEB SERVICES

Christopher Strauber

Cloud computing is not so much one concept as it is a set of related developments in computer technology and networking, combined with a set of ideas about how those technologies and networks can be used to solve problems. It is heavily in use as a marketing buzzword and often applied to almost any new technology or service related to the Web. The ongoing conversation in the IT industry about what it means and how it applies is confusing and highly technical, but several main directions and applications are clearly relevant for libraries. Some of the issues raised by cloud computing, like remote storage and related privacy concerns, are not new to libraries at all. A few definitions are in order. Based on the definitions, I will describe some examples of current business and personal applications of cloud computing that will point to trends and tools libraries can watch for and use.

DEFINITIONS

The term "cloud computing" derives from the typical representation of the Internet in diagrams of how networked computer systems operate. The actual complexity of the interconnected systems required, for example, to send an e-mail from an Internet cafe in Prague and have it arrive at your home computer is hard to represent concisely. But since the network of several layers of connected computers on multiple continents can be expected to do its job reliably, the exact steps the e-mail message takes on its way from point A to point B are something of an academic point from the user's perspective. Representing this complexity by simply drawing a cloud labeled "Internet" or "Web" in the appropriate part of the flowchart is now a common convention among network engineers and software designers. In this sense, the cloud is a black box into and out of which various sorts of information flow.

More practically, the definition depends on one's perspective. A corporate information technology manager might see it as a way of saving money and staff time by paying for storage and maintenance she would otherwise have to do herself. Engineers at Google might see it as the cornerstone of their search empire, which uses an enormous number of cheap computers to do computational work beyond the power of the largest supercomputers. A college student might see an online word processor, which allows him to save one copy of his term paper to a Web site and access it from any computer with Internet access. A marketing expert might see it as a concept trendy and amorphous enough to allow it to be applied to almost anything, as the CEO of Oracle (Larry Ellison) is widely quoted as saying. Richard Stallman, a proponent of free software and personal freedom, sees it as a threat to both of those things, a way for giant companies to take even more control over one's personal life and data (Johnson 2008).

The inclusive definition used here is that of Aaron Weiss, writing for *net-Worker*, who sees cloud computing as a combination of distributed computing, remote storage, and web services that users can access from anywhere (2007). As noted above, depending on the perspective of the person discussing it, one or more of the aspects of cloud computing can seem more important than the others. But these three categories cover most of the discussion of cloud computing one is likely to see.

The basic idea of distributed computing is that a large enough network of cheap computers can do the work formerly done by huge supercomputers at great expense. The advantage of this approach is that hardware problems are not much of a concern with a large network. If the single supercomputer fails, everything fails. If one computer in a network of 10,000 fails, the loss in productivity is imperceptible. A nontechnical example would be a 10,000-person-hour project. For one person this would be several years' work but, assuming the parts of the project could be adequately broken down into small tasks, as more staff are hired the time and attention required by each team member is less.

The classic example of remote storage is the collection of family photos likely sitting on a hard drive somewhere in your home right now. Since hard drives fail with some regularity, most serious photographers make backup copies. But lots of people who diligently make backups keep the backups in the house, so if there were a fire or some other natural disaster, both original and backup would be lost. Many people solve this problem by making a copy and keeping it in a safe- deposit box, or with a friend. The cloud computing version of this is to make a digital copy and save it on someone else's computer, most likely belonging to a company selling the disk space.

Web services (the corporate term is "Software as a Service" or SaaS) is the third key area. Typically built using distributed computing and remote storage, web services provide through a Web site the sorts of tools typically used through a program installed on one's own computer. A wide variety of online services provide e-mail, word processors and spreadsheets, calendars, photo and video sharing, and, in fact, almost everything else typically done with a home computer. This is the user perspective on the cloud: a service which can be used from any computer or other device with an Internet connection, frequently available at no cost or supported by advertising.

DISTRIBUTED COMPUTING

Three concrete examples will serve to illustrate how distributed computing works in practice. According to Weiss, instead of taking the traditional approach to computing on a massive scale, building one mammoth data center with an expensive supercomputer, Google's founders chose to use a very large number of cheap and interchangeable commodity computers that combined could perform as well or better than a single supercomputer ... and with much less risk of failure. Weiss estimates that Google runs approximately half a million computer servers in more than a dozen locations worldwide to operate the various parts of its business (2007).

A simpler example of the power of distributed computing is the SETI@ Home Project, run by the University of California, Berkeley. The SETI project attempts to analyze radio waves in space for evidence of alien life. Given that there is a vast amount of electromagnetic noise to filter through, even the data produced by one radio telescope requires a massive amount of computing power to manage. SETI@Home encourages home computer users to download software that allows their computer's spare processing power to be linked with that of other users to analyze the data. It was originally hoped that 50,000 people would participate; almost three million do. No extraterrestrial life has been found as of yet, but several areas for further research have been identified (SETI@Home).

Amazon, the web retailer, has also been in the position of needing to build a huge network of computers to run its business. In 2006 Amazon began to sell metered access to its vast computing resources through Amazon Web Services. This addressed a major problem with traditional approaches to providing computing power, the problem of predicting demand for a web service. A company running its own computer servers and setting up a Web site has to make an estimate of how much demand there will be for the service. If the estimate is too low and the site suddenly becomes very popular, it takes time to build and install new hardware ... time during which potential customers would be lost. If the estimate is too high, a large amount of expensive equipment would sit idle most of the time. By, in essence, offering its excess computer capacity as a utility through its Elastic Compute Cloud

(EC2) service, Amazon allows companies to build only what they need at the moment, secure in the knowledge that quick expansion is available, and also sure that they will only pay for what they actually use.

REMOTE STORAGE

A second major part of Amazon's set of web services is its Simple Storage Service, or S3. Using distributed computing, it offers unlimited storage on a pay-as-you-go basis. Users pay an extremely modest price per gigabyte of storage used per month, with prices declining as more storage is added. Users also pay for the cost of transferring data in and out of the service.

Some scale references are helpful. A gigabyte is the storage space required for a few hundred standard-sized music files, or about the same number of text-only electronic books; *War and Peace* is about the same size, three megabytes, as the average music track. Using Lyman and Varian's estimates, if the approximately 19 million items in the Library of Congress were digitized, they would take up about 10 terabytes of space (2003). Amazon S3's top bracket for storage pricing starts at 500 terabytes per month. This means it is designed for almost unimaginably vast amounts of data.

Comparative pricing is also a relevant consideration. A recent *Wall Street Journal* article estimated the cost for businesses of storing business-critical data on hard disks to be $30–$40 per gigabyte, while saving it to tape backups costs approximately $.40 per gigabyte (Lawton 2008). The potential cost savings alone change the dynamics of data-oriented businesses. For consumers, a one-terabyte hard drive costs approximately $100–$200, or $.10 to $.20 per gigabyte (at Newegg.com, 3/22/2009)—but without the additional advantages of being off-site, or of being protected by multiple redundant backups, or of professional data center management. Amazon currently charges $.15 per gigabyte per month up to 50 terabytes, with prices declining as more storage is added. Data transfer costs are currently $.10 per gigabyte uploaded, and $.17 per gigabyte transferred out (Amazon Simple Storage Service 2009).

Several companies compete to offer this sort of service to businesses, including Rackspace and many, many others. There are also consumer-level backup services like Mozy and Carbonite, which use remote storage to create backup copies of data on personal computers.

Google's Sam Schillace has such confidence in Google's remote storage that he periodically offers to reformat his hard drive if the reporter he is talking to will do so as well (Agger 2009). Reformatting the hard drive, if you have stored your information locally and do not have a good backup elsewhere, means destroying everything on your computer. No one has accepted the offer.

From a purely pragmatic perspective, cheap storage which is accessible from anywhere should be an obvious choice. But storing data on someone else's computers immediately raises a variety of privacy and security issues to which there are only incomplete solutions so far. According to the Electronic Frontier Foundation, electronic communications like e-mail, voice messages, text messages, and so forth have some level of protection and privacy under federal law, but data stored with a third party can typically be obtained by the government with only a subpoena rather than a search warrant. EFF recommends that private information be kept locally, or at least that any private information sent to an outside service be encrypted. Note: this is possible to do with data sent to Amazon S3, and it is part of the service provided by Mozy and Carbonite (Electronic Frontier Foundation 2009).

Privacy concerns are obviously a serious matter for libraries, but it is worth considering that many very large businesses trust cloud services to manage huge amounts of proprietary, extremely valuable, and traditionally very private data. Salesforce.com, which primarily sells a cloud-based Customer Relationship Management service, had over 55,000 business customers and $289 million in revenue in the fourth quarter of 2008—up 34 percent from 2007 (Weier 2009). These systems typically manage information about a company's current, past, and potential customers, information that most businesses guard zealously. The question, then, would be which library data require more safeguards than that.

WEB SERVICES

From the perspective of the IT manager or the programmer, the cloud is a connected set of computers working together to provide large amounts of storage and power. From the perspective of the user, the cloud is the products and services built with those tools and, for many, the work-anywhere style of computing that they make possible.

Making vast amounts of computing power and storage available on the Internet has made it possible to create a variety of new services, some of which compete with existing computer software in features ... and usually definitively beat it on price. Software as a Service (often abbreviated SaaS) lets the user visit a Web site to do things he or she would previously have done using a purchased piece of software. E-mail, word processing, spreadsheets, calendars, even photo editing, and storage are now available online.

E-mail was the first major piece of personal software to be widely available online, whether through Yahoo or Microsoft's Hotmail or later through Google's Gmail. Anyone who has tried to keep versions of Outlook or some other e-mail program synchronized between work, home, and a laptop will immediately understand how hard it is to keep straight which messages have been answered and which have not, and how easy it is to lose track of vital messages. Or, perhaps closer to home, imagine a reference librarian working at several different computers during the day who wants to have access to both new and saved messages from wherever she is. Webmail solves the problem of synchronization by keeping the data in one place on the Web, which the user can get to from any computer with an Internet connection. Additionally, "computer" is increasingly coming to mean a very wide array of devices, from desktops to laptops to mobile phones and iPods.

Though not the first online office suite or by any means the only one—there are a dozen major competitors—Google Docs can serve as a model of a web service offered in place of (wholly or partially) software that most people consider critical to computing: word processing, spreadsheets, and presentations. Users log into their Google accounts, create their documents online, and save them online. It is possible, but not necessary, to save a copy on the computer one is working at. The features are similar to those in commercial software, and it is for the moment a free service for Google account holders.

This has several advantages: (1) It reduces the need to worry about where the copy of the conference presentation is, as one can simply log into Google and retrieve it. (2) It makes it much easier to share and collaborate on documents. Since the document is a web page, potential collaborators can be sent a link rather than a document, and it is possible for several people to edit a document at once. (3) Google Docs saves each succeeding version of the document and archives all of them, making it extremely easy to return to a previous version. (4) Google can continuously improve the product without requiring users to buy a new version.

Web services have the same main disadvantage of remote storage, the lack of predictable privacy. Placing potentially sensitive personal or business information on someone else's computer is something many would not be comfortable with, and which may raise legal questions for certain types of organizations and records. Additionally, both Google and Amazon have had widely publicized service outages in the last six months. Both incidents lasted a few hours but were enough to generate a variety of media reports on whether cloud services are reliable (Nuttall 2009).

LIBRARY APPLICATIONS

Most libraries have already taken a major step into cloud computing and the advantages and complexities it adds. Over the last 10 to 15 years it has become normal for libraries to spend large percentages of their collection budgets on access to journal, magazine, and newspaper articles hosted on vendor Web sites. According to the National Center for Educational Statistics, academic libraries alone spent over $700 million on electronic serials in 2006 (Holton et al. 2008). Access versus ownership, an old conversation in collection development circles, is in that sense a cloud computing issue. For the most part, users get the benefits of cloud services: access everywhere and a service which works on any sort of computer. Libraries get the benefit of professional management of storage and web hosting.

Another current trend to watch is the cloud library catalog. Innovative Interfaces' Encore system and WorldCat Local are both in essence cloud services. Ex Libris has a similar hosted service, as do the open source ILS systems, Equinox and Koha. There is no more central function for libraries than the catalog, and for that to become a subscription service rather than a piece of self-maintained infrastructure marks an extremely large shift.

LibGuides is another example of a core library function, the creation and display of research guides, which many libraries are opting to buy as a service rather than build themselves.

For libraries, as for other sorts of organizations, there is a legitimate question about which functions need to be managed in-house and which can reasonably be handled more cheaply and efficiently by others. As universities stop providing e-mail service to students (Young 2008) and close their computer labs (Kolowich 2009), libraries too may wish to ask whether there are more appropriate ways to handle traditional services.

THREE LONG-TERM TRENDS TO WATCH

Managing Large Data Sets

Managing very large amounts of digital data is something libraries are likely to be involved in, if in fact they are not already. Again, for comparative scale, the Internet Archive recently set up a new modular data center to store and manage its three petabytes of ever-growing data. Using the comparison from earlier, that is more or less equivalent to 150 Libraries of Congress (Stokes 2009). As similarly large amounts of data in the sciences and social sciences are collected and organized for preservation (Lynch 2008), libraries will necessarily be involved in the process. Lynch also sagely points out that the entire cultural record of mankind is the relevant data set for researchers in the humanities. Management and curation on that scale will require cooperative agreements, pooled resources, and national, if not global, planning. It will also require a flexible and infinitely expandable set of computing resources. Project Bamboo, an exploratory project designed to facilitate cooperation and shared resources in the digital humanities, is discussing a cloud infrastructure as one possible model ("Shared Services" 2009).

Remote Storage for Preservation

The personal arguments for remote storage mentioned previously apply even more forcefully to libraries and archives, which are responsible for permanent preservation of our collective cultural heritage. As part of a systematic disaster plan, professionally managed off-site storage seems like one very reasonable approach to mitigating the risks inherent in fragile collections and fragile buildings.

Simplifying Computer Maintenance and Reducing Software Costs

As cloud services like Google Docs become more prevalent and more widely used, it may be possible for libraries to simplify their public PCs. If the web browser becomes the primary means of access to everything, arguments against free computer operating systems like Linux become harder to sustain. Also, the computer hardware required to run a web browser is much less expensive. This is the model of computing of the new "netbook," a small and inexpensive laptop computer designed primarily to use web services for things normally done on the computer itself. Introduced in 2007, 14 million were sold last year (Stokes 2008). Simple, easily replaced computers that primarily run web services are worth considering for many sorts of libraries.

CONCLUSION

Given a fast Internet connection and the speed with which modern computers work, a computer in the next room and a computer on the other side of the world are essentially the same distance apart. Computers linked inside an office share a network; computers linked by the Internet also share a network. Increasingly the distinction between software run on one's own computer and software run on a Web site is arbitrary. The Internet, in some senses, is one giant computer to which almost every other computing device is connected ("What Is Cloud Computing" 2008 at 5:19).

The term "cloud computing" may cease to be a buzzword. That would probably be a blessing. But the technology it describes, distributed computing and remote storage, and the services built with it, are already shaping the future of libraries.

REFERENCES

Agger, Michael. "Kill Your Computer and Join the Cloud." *Slate*, March 2, 2009. http://www.slate.com/id/2212467/ (accessed March 2, 2009).

Amazon Simple Storage Service (Amazon S3). http://aws.amazon.com/s3/#pricing (accessed March 22, 2009).

Electronic Frontier Foundation. "Online Storage of Your Private Data." *Surveillance Self-Defense*. https://ssd.eff.org/3rdparties/protect/storage (accessed May 14, 2009).

Holton, Barbara, Laura Hardesty, and Patricia O'Shea. *Academic Libraries: 2006. First Look (NCES 2008–337)*. Washington, DC: National Center for Education Statistics, Institute of Education Sciences, U.S. Department of Education, 2008. http://nces.ed.gov/pubsearch/pubsinfo.asp?pubid=2008337 (accessed March 27, 2009).

Johnson, Bobbie. "Cloud Computing Is a Trap, Warns GNU Founder." *Guardian,* September 29, 2008. http://www.guardian.co.uk/technology/2008/sep/ 29/cloud.computing.richard.stallman (accessed March 21, 2009).

Kolowich, Steve. "U. of Virginia Plans to Phase Out Public Computer Labs." *The Wired Campus,* March 23, 2009. http://chronicle.com/wiredcampus/article/ 3676/u-virginia-plans-to-phase-out-public-computer-labs (accessed March 29, 2009).

"Larry Ellison—What The Hell Is Cloud Computing?" September 27, 2008. http:// www.youtube.com/watch?v=0FacYAI6DY0 (accessed March 21, 2009).

Lawton, Christopher. "Running Out of Room." *Wall Street Journal,* September 29, 2008: R.9.

Lyman, Peter and Hal R. Varian. "How Much Information 2003?" October 27, 2003. http://www2.sims.berkeley.edu/research/projects/how-much-info-2003/index.htm (accessed March 22, 2009).

Lynch, Clifford. "The Institutional Challenges of Cyberinfrastructure and E-Research." *Educause Review* 43, no. 6 (2008). http://connect.educause.edu/Library/ EDUCAUSE+Review/TheInstitutionalChallenge/47446 (accessed March 28, 2009).

Nuttall, Chris. "Google E-mail Crash Hits Millions and Raises Fears over Web Services." *Financial Times,* February 25, 2009. http://www.ft.com/cms/ s/0/0950a2b6–02de-11de-b58b-000077b07658.html (accessed May 14, 2009).

SETI@Home. http://en.wikipedia.org/wiki/SETI@home (accessed March 22, 2009). (Note: Wikipedia here accurately summarizes several pages of the SETI@Home Web site.)

"Shared Services—Program Document Sec 4—Discussion Draft of 9 March 2009." https://wiki.projectbamboo.org/display/BPUB/Shared+Services+-+ Program+Document+Sec+4+-+Discussion+Draft+of+9+March+2009 (accessed March 28, 2009).

Stokes, John. "Netbook Sales Surge in Economic Downturn; Where's Apple?" *ars technica,* December 21, 2008. http://arstechnica.com/apple/news/2008/12/net book-sales-surge-in-economic-downturn-wheres-apple.ars (accessed March 28, 2009).

Stokes, John. "Sun Puts Internet Archive in a Box, But Will It Stay There?" *ars technica,* March 27, 2009. http://arstechnica.com/web/news/2009/03/sun-puts-internet-archive-in-a-box-but-will-it-stay-there.ars (accessed March 28, 2009).

Weier, Mary Hayes. "Salesforce.com's Growth Shows SaaS Success In Tough Economy." *InformationWeek,* February 26, 2009. http://www.informationweek. com/news/services/saas/showArticle.jhtml?articleID=214600343 (accessed May 14, 2009).

Weiss, Aaron. "Computing in the Clouds. *netWorker* 11, no. 4 (2007): 16–25.

"What is Cloud Computing." May 7, 2008. http://www.youtube.com/watch?v= 6PNuQHUiV3Q (accessed March 14, 2009).

Young, Jeffrey. "Boston College Will Stop Offering New Students E-Mail Accounts." *The Wired Campus,* November 19, 2008. http://chronicle.com/wiredcampus/ article/3473/boston-college-to-stop-offering-student-e-mail-accounts-to-freshmen-starting-next-year (accessed March 29, 2009).

ADDITIONAL READING

Johnson, L., A. Levine, and R. Smith. *Horizon Report*. Austin, Texas: New Media Consortium, 2009. http://connect.educause.edu/Library/ELI/2009Horizon Report/48003.

4

LEARNING MANAGEMENT SYSTEMS

Kim Duckett

Since the late 1990s the use of technologies to support teaching and learning has become increasingly commonplace in education. No longer is online learning tightly associated with "distance education" or "distance learning." Increasingly, much of the learning taking place in schools, colleges, and universities has some component of online activity, and learning management systems are frequently at the center of this online learning. The names of learning management systems such as Blackboard, Desire2Learn, Moodle, and Sakai are now common in education.

Learning management systems (LMSs) are also frequently called course management systems (CMSs—not to be confused with "content management systems"), or courseware. They are suites of teaching technologies that make it easier for instructors to create and maintain online course materials. LMSs typically include a variety of tools for creating course content such as web pages, online syllabi, collections of readings, and links to Web sites. They allow users to store files directly in the system as well as link out to files on external servers. Integrated communication tools—discussion boards, e-mail, a built-in calendar, and online chat—facilitate both synchronous and asynchronous communication between instructors and learners. Increasingly, such systems include blogs and wikis to enhance collaboration. Instructors can use online quizzes and exams to assess learning, and students submit their assignments using the LMS and view their grades online. Instructors may teach an entire course online through an LMS or use specific tools to supplement and support face-to-face instruction.

In addition to the suites of instructional tools built into the LMS, many learning management systems have some way for external partners to develop applications that extend the LMS's functionality. Programmers at commercial companies or at educational institutions can use a software development kit (SDK) provided by the LMS vendor, which enables the creation of interoperable products that connect to the learning management system. For example, Blackboard has "Building Blocks" and "Power Links" designed by external companies in order to enrich the suite of learning technologies at the hands of instructors in the LMS. A commercial "Building Block" or "Power Link" might focus on connecting students to a synchronous online classroom, a more full-featured quizzing tool than the one built into Blackboard, or a plagiarism detection program. Local programmers might also use the SDK in order to create their own applications. Commercial companies are not only targeting Blackboard and other for-profit learning management companies; certain companies are also creating integration points between their products and Moodle and Sakai.

The use of learning management systems in higher education has become pervasive. The *EDUCAUSE Core Data Survey*, which tracks campus information technology environments and practices, reports that 93 percent of the 994 higher education institutions that completed the 2007 survey currently have at least one LMS in use on campus (EDUCAUSE Core Data Service 2007). Some institutions, especially large research universities, have multiple LMS options for faculty. The survey also found that on 64.9 percent of reporting campuses, faculty use the LMS selectively, although at 35.1 percent of the institutions, the LMS is used for nearly every course. Additionally, according to the 2008 *ECAR Study of Undergraduate Students and Information Technology*, of the more than 27,000 respondents, 82.3 percent have used an LMS (Salaway and Caruso 2008).

Today there are a number of commercial and open source LMSs on the market. In 2006 Blackboard Inc. acquired WebCT, making it the largest LMS company in the world. Although there is technically no longer a product line called WebCT, some people who were using WebCT products still refer to their LMS as WebCT rather than calling it by its Blackboard name. According to the 2007 *EDUCAUSE Core Data Survey*, 66.3 percent of reporting institutions use a Blackboard/WebCT product (EDUCAUSE Core Data Service 2007). Desire2Learn and Angel are two other noteworthy commercial learning management systems.

Since commercial LMSs are expensive and have less flexibility for customizing the product to local needs, open source LMSs such as Moodle and Sakai are growing in popularity. Moodle (Modular Object-Oriented Dynamic Learning Environment) is a free open source LMS that is growing in popularity. It has an active development community with global participation. The Sakai Project is an outgrowth of collaboration among Stanford University, the University of Michigan, Indiana University, the Massachusetts

Institute of Technology, and the University of California at Berkeley. Like Moodle, developers at institutions around the world are adapting Sakai to local needs as well as sharing open source code among the broader user community. According to the *National Survey of Information Technology in U.S. Higher Education* (Campus Computing Project 2008), 24.4 percent of respondents report a high likelihood that their institution would migrate to an open source LMS within the next five years.

BRINGING THE LIBRARY INTO THE LMS: TECHNICAL AND CULTURAL CHALLENGES

As adoption of LMSs in higher education has grown, many libraries have actively sought to define a presence in these virtual spaces in order to connect with faculty and students where teaching and learning is taking place. Instructional support is one of the core services and values of the library, and as the LMS becomes increasingly central to instruction, it is important for libraries to find ways to support users in this online environment.

There are two primary strategies associated with integration between the library and the LMS: (1) *system level integration* that strives for a pervasive library presence throughout the LMS and (2) *course level support* that builds on partnerships between librarians and instructors. In their book *Academic Librarianship by Design,* Bell and Shank (2007) provide a useful overview of these two strategies, which they term the "system level" and "course level" approaches, respectively. In both cases, collaboration is at the heart of the integration. The system level approach can take a variety of forms, but typically involves collaboration between LMS administrators, programmers, and librarians to develop technical solutions. Course level support necessitates cooperation between librarians and instructors working together on a specific course as well as librarians creating stand-alone training materials to aid faculty as they incorporate library resources into the LMS on their own. At many institutions, librarians are approaching the LMS from both the high level system and more grassroots course levels. Additionally, a librarian might actually serve as the instructor for a whole information literacy course and use the LMS in a teaching capacity.

Librarians have been pointing out the lack of a library presence in courseware since the early 2000s. The title of Cohen's 2002 article in *EDUCAUSE Review,* in fact, asked the right question: "Course-Management Software: Where's the Library?" This question was also tackled by the IMS Global Learning Consortium and the Coalition of Networked Information (McLean and Lynch 2004) and the Digital Library Federation (Flecker and McLean 2004), all of which explored issues of interoperability and opportunities for the connection between LMSs and libraries.

As Gibbons (2005) describes in her *Library Technology Report* on course management systems, there are both technical and cultural barriers to the integration of the library into LMSs. One important technical barrier is the number and variety of information silos libraries own, license, and maintain. The diversity of these silos makes it difficult to design a system that allows students and faculty to search easily for library resources from within the LMS itself. Another challenge is the difficulty of creating persistent URLs to journal articles through online subscriptions. The instability of these links makes it challenging for faculty to link to readings from within their online syllabi or assignments within the LMS, and most instructors and students have no concept that many journal article links break after a certain amount of time. The technical architecture of the learning management system can also prohibit seamless integration between library resources such as article databases, the library catalog, and online journals. This last problem often means that students have to log in once to the LMS and then again to library resources or juggle between using the LMS and accessing the library's resources in multiple browser windows. Additionally, the technical infrastructure of certain learning management systems prohibits or makes it extremely difficult to develop any kind of automated integration. As a result, in some LMSs any integration of links to library resources must be done by hand even if an automatic integration is desirable.

Furthermore, there are cultural barriers to the integration of the library into the LMS (Gibbons 2005). Learning management systems can be run by a variety of campus units, including central information technology, learning technology services, academic colleges, or the library. When the LMS is run by a unit external to the library, the development of technical solutions to connect the library's resources to the LMS may require collaboration between campus organizations without historic partnerships. On some campuses there might even be tension between the library and such units. Furthermore, because librarians have not frequently been involved in campus decisions about learning technology purchases, commercial LMS vendors have not viewed libraries as important stakeholders in the development of their products and services.

As librarians seek to partner with instructors to include library content in courses within the LMS they may also face a general misperception by faculty about the role of librarians and the scope of how they can support student learning. Although librarians are frequently successful in collaboration with faculty, there are instructors who may not recognize the value in allowing librarians access to their online course sites in order to incorporate library resources. As a result, a library's effort to include a library presence in the LMS requires librarians to convey to stakeholders the value of putting library resources and instruction at the students' fingertips as part of the course materials. In order to articulate this value, librarians need to be familiar with how to use learning management systems and consider the LMS a natural extension of the library. Since online course environments have not historically been an environment in which librarians operate, use of LMSs is not a natural activity for many librarians. In fact, a survey of librarians in the California State University system found that those who received training on how to use a learning management system were not more likely to collaborate with faculty to include information literacy in courses in the LMS (Jackson 2007).

SYSTEM LEVEL INTEGRATION

The system level approach to integration between the library and the LMS often focuses on the development of technical solutions to create a library presence as part of the infrastructure of the LMS. It can also result in the creation of embedded tools that enable instructors and librarians to incorporate links to course pages or guides, readings and/or databases, and online journals directly into courses. The depth of integration and the amount of customization to courses vary. Library content may be targeted at the campus-wide level (all courses) or more tailored to curricula (i.e., academic departments) or specific courses.

Global Library Presence

Within certain learning management systems it is possible for systems administrators to insert a tab, button, or link into the global navigation of the LMS, which takes users to targeted information and tools. A common example is the Blackboard "library tab" built into the interface of the LMS and dedicated to library content. This kind of integration usually requires that the library advocate for a pervasive presence in the LMS and work closely with the campus unit that runs it. Clicking on the Blackboard "library tab" often takes the user to the library's home page framed within the LMS or another Web site put together by the library and highlighting resources for students. A Blackboard "library tab" customized beyond a link to the library's home page may include access points to the library catalog, article databases, instructional materials, library information, and a search option for electronic reserves. The Roosevelt University Blackboard "library tab," for instance, highlights the library's instant messaging and e-mail reference service, research guides, writing and citation tools, services for distance learners, and tips for connecting to the library from off campus. Students can also read announcements from the library's blog. The library's home page is a click away (see figure 4.1).

Since the "library tab" is built into the global navigation of the LMS, the content is accessible to all users and becomes an integral part of the LMS. This kind of global presence necessitates that the content accessed via the tab, button, or link is generic enough to span across all courses and learning scenarios. The benefit of such a solution is that the library has a pervasive presence throughout the LMS. Its weakness is that the library content must serve all users and is therefore not tailored to the specific needs of different courses.

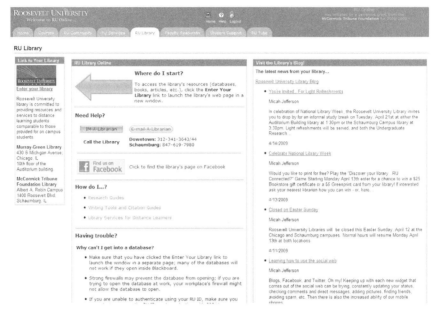

Figure 4.1. Roosevelt University Blackboard Library Tab.
Roosevelt University.

Curriculum and Course Level Technical Integration

At some institutions libraries are working with campus partners who manage the LMS to provide access to library resources and content targeted towards the discipline of the course or specifically tailored to the course. In such cases, libraries rely on course data such as curriculum codes (ex. ENG) and course numbers (ex. 101) to match library resources to specific courses based around disciplinary areas or "course pages" of recommendations designed by subject specialist librarians. Duke University Libraries, for example, has a "Library Guides" link in the left sidebar navigation of Blackboard. When a student clicks on the link, a disciplinary focused subject guide is launched in a new window. Librarians can also tailor the guide to specific assignments in the course.

The Rochester Institute of Technology Libraries' "Library Resources Link Server" is a locally developed web-based application that uses course data to match library resources to specific courses in the LMS Desire2Learn (Rochester Institute of Technology Libraries). The end result is a "myLibrary" link that appears any time a student logs into the LMS. The "myLibrary" link takes the user to a set of resources tailored to the curriculum or course. Subject specialist librarians can create information for courses at the college, academic department, or course level. The technical infrastructure of the system is designed so that the most customized content is matched to the "myLibrary" instance for any given course. The "Library Resources Link Server" also has a faculty view that provides instructors with links to services of benefit to faculty such as reserves and distance learning library services.

Using the Moodle software development kit, programmers at North Carolina State University Libraries have similarly created a Moodle "block," which leverages course data for a particular course section in order to provide access to a variety of library resources and services from within the course itself. The Moodle block is part of NCSU's Library Course Views Project (branded Library Tools), an application that dynamically generates student-centric views of library resources and tools for all courses taught at NCSU (Casden et al. 2009). The "Library Tools block" offers one-click access to the electronic reserves for the course section, disciplinary article databases, the library catalog, recommendations created by subject specialist librarians, and links to library services such as virtual reference. Programmers in the library worked with LMS administrators to create the "Library Tools block," which is a permanent part of the suite of tools in the LMS. Instructors can easily insert the block and thereby create a dynamic link from the course in the LMS to the course-specific Library Tools page on the library's server (see figure 4.2).

Like the Rochester Institute of Technology's system, NCSU's Library Course Views system balances broad coverage of courses with customized content for different courses by allowing librarians to design recommendations tailored to colleges, curricula, courses, and course sections. Similar work has been

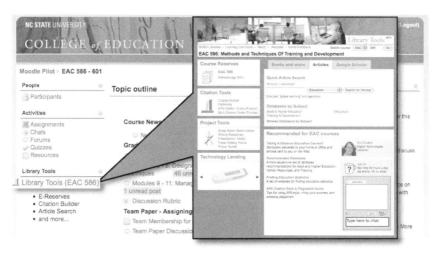

Figure 4.2. NCSU Library Tools Moodle block (left) with corresponding Library Tools page for course.

Used with permission of North Carolina State University; ©North Carolina State University 2009.

done at the Ohio State University Libraries as part of its Learning Management System "Toolkit" in Desire2Learn (Black 2008). Using various levels of content customization enables the library to enhance the appropriateness of library resources for different courses in a way that a generic library tab, button, or link in the LMS cannot achieve. This strategy is appealing because it strives to balance broad coverage of courses in the LMS with the tailoring of library content to the varying disciplinary and instructional needs of different courses.

Reserves as Part of the LMS

Electronic reserves have become a staple service in many academic libraries. Since instructors often use the LMS to provide their students with online access to assignments and readings for the course, the connection between electronic reserves maintained by the library and the learning management system is a natural intersection. The authentication required to access courses in the LMS also helps libraries securely connect students to copyrighted materials. In most cases, the library continues to use the catalog and library servers to manage reserve items, while helping instructors insert links to the readings within the LMS. The Ohio State University Libraries actually stores and manages reserve items within their learning management system Desire2Learn (Black 2008). An institution can also use Blackboard's Content Management System product, which can be licensed in tandem with the LMS Blackboard Academic Suite, to store and manage reserves.

Sakaibrary

Under a grant from the Andrew W. Mellon Foundation, Indiana University and the University of Michigan have collaborated on the development of open source software tools that facilitate the integration of library-licensed digital content within Sakai (Indiana University Digital Library Program). This important project focuses on empowering faculty with tools built into Sakai that enable them to search for and link to licensed resources paid for by their institution's library. The Citations Helper tool allows users to search Google Scholar and/or a library metasearch engine from within Sakai and import scholarly, licensed content into their courses in the LMS. Users can also import citations from Refworks or EndNote accounts. After selecting content, instructors can make citation lists and link them to syllabi, assignments, announcements, or the class schedule. Additionally, a Research Guides tool enables librarians and/or instructors to build annotated sets of library resources directly into the Sakai course site. These guides are similar to the "course pages" or "course guides" many librarians create on their library's Web site. Unlike these other library web pages, however, the research guides in Sakai are seamlessly built into the course (see figure 4.3).

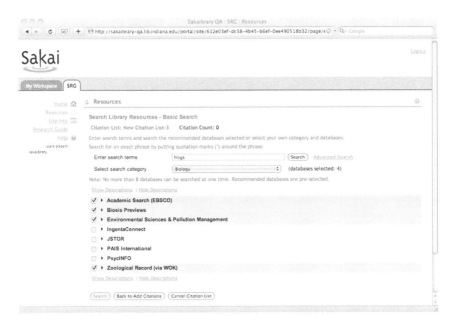

Figure 4.3. Sakaibrary's Citation Helper.

Indiana University, 2009.

System Level Integration: Benefits and Challenges

An important benefit of developing a technical integration between the library and the LMS is that it provides users with a convenient way to access the library's resources and services. Giving students access points to library subscription-based electronic resources close to course content enables them to become aware of and make use of the variety of search tools and resources provided by the library. Additionally, as Bell and Shank (2007) point out, the library's presence in the LMS increases visibility of the library and enforces its relevance in teaching and learning. They also suggest that the integration of existing library content and services into the LMS saves staff time. It expands the work of librarians beyond the library's Web site.

Technical integration requires development time as well as healthy collaboration between librarians and LMS administrators, both of which can be challenging. It can also be difficult to balance extensive course coverage with the tailoring of content to specific course needs. At the same time Bell and Shank (2007) suggest that there may be a disadvantage in providing a pervasive library presence in the LMS because it can lead to a loss of face-to-face connection between librarians and students.

Another important challenge to recognize is that LMSs may come and go. WebCT was acquired by Blackboard. A campus may migrate from one LMS to another. Any technical development targeted towards a given LMS means that resources are being directed towards a solution that may not transfer to another system. As a result, technical projects involving LMSs should consider the longevity of the system on campus.

COURSE LEVEL PARTNERSHIPS AND SUPPORT

In addition to efforts to create tools and strategies for technical integration between the library and LMSs on a large scale, librarians are actively partnering with instructors and other instructional support staff (i.e., learning technologists, instructional designers) on a course-by-course level to include library resources, services, and instructional content. Unlike the system level approach, course level partnerships are built on personal relationships and require the creation of more librarian-authored web content and links added to the LMS manually. The Sakaibrary project, however, spans the technical and course level partnership strategies because it has involved the technical development of specific tools to facilitate the insertion of content into the LMS by instructors and librarians.

Bell and Shank (2007) present a variety of strategies for librarians to provide library- research assistance more tailored to specific courses. For example, librarians can work with instructors to:

- Provide a library instruction session outline students can access before or after a librarian meets with the class
- Create customized course pages and assignment guides
- Insert links to library resources such as article databases and journals as well as external Web sites
- Use the assessment tools built into the LMS to gather pre- and posttest quiz data as part of information literacy assessment
- Maintain a library- or research-related discussion board monitored by the librarian

In order to facilitate the inclusion of information literacy instruction in the LMS through librarian-faculty collaboration, Jackson (2007) offers suggestions such as designating a library LMS liaison, creating partnerships with the LMS administrator and learning technologists, and encouraging librarian training in use of the LMS. She also recommends designing Web sites, tutorials, and handouts so they can easily be reused in multiple courses.

In recent years the term "embedded librarian" has become associated with this kind of close collaboration between librarians and instructors through in-depth involvement in the course. For example, the Public Services Librarian and the Coordinator of Academic Services Online at Community College of Vermont, Brattleboro, closely partnered to embed a librarian's presence in online distance education courses (Matthew and Schroeder 2006). As a "teaching assistant" the librarian is able to participate in a discussion forum pertaining to research assignments and use the announcements feature to connect to students. The students can ask the librarian questions about their research topics on a discussion board and he or she responds with suggestions such as appropriate databases or good keywords. The librarian can also post useful search strategies and citation tips that will be beneficial for all students. Due to heavy marketing by the library, the program grew from two courses in spring 2004 to 43 courses in spring 2006.

Guides to Help Instructors Include Library Resources in the LMS

Some instructors may not want a librarian to be a member of their course in the LMS, feel it is unnecessary, or not realize this option is available. Nonetheless, they may still need help in properly linking to online journal articles and databases due to the instability of URLs associated with electronic resources. As a result, certain libraries provide web-based guides that highlight ideas for including library resources and provide instruction in how to integrate links to library resources such as article databases and e-journals on their own, including how to set up links to work from both on and off campus through the library's proxy server. These guides often also promote the library's range of instructional support such as e-reserves, virtual reference, and various instructional guides (i.e., citing sources, evaluating information).

Course Level Integration: Strengths and Challenges

One of the major strengths of librarian involvement with a course in the LMS is that it allows librarians to extend or supplement the "one-shot" library instruction session they provide to students as part of the class. It enables the librarian to have an ongoing relationship with the course and, in some cases, such as through activity on the discussion board, to provide additional research assistance for the students. By collaborating closely with the faculty, the librarian may become an important instructional support partner, which can lead to the instructor turning to the librarian for additional strategies to deepen student learning.

A challenge librarians face in working closely with courses in LMSs is that they must be added to the course section in order to interact with the course materials or to connect to students. In most cases, faculty must grant the librarian access to the course, but there is typically no designation for "librarian" among the user roles. As a result, librarians have to use a role such as "designer" that distinguishes them from "instructors" but may not properly describe their involvement in the course. In some LMSs students can view participants in the course by their role, and they may misunderstand the librarian's role if it is designated as "designer" rather than "librarian." The Ohio State University Libraries (Black 2008) has been able to work with LMS administrators at their campus to create a specially designated "librarian" role in Desire2Learn.

A major weakness in course level integration built on partnerships between librarians and instructors is that such work can be time-consuming when librarians are successful in marketing their services. It takes a lot of time and effort to create resource guides tailored to specific courses and to help many instructors with different courses in the LMS. Additionally, these guides and links to resources tailored for the course must be maintained over time, adding to the staff work involved. As a result, while the course level approach can certainly enrich courses, it is difficult to scale the library's efforts and reach many courses with this strategy, especially at large institutions.

CONCLUSION

The examples of system level and course level integration highlighted in this chapter constitute only a small sample of projects that forge a connection between the library and learning management systems. Despite possible technical, political, and cultural barriers that might exist, librarians at many institutions continue to work towards meaningful partnerships with LMS administrators, instructors, and other campus instructional support staff to establish a presence for the library in these critical online learning environments. Such integration offers students easier access to the library, closely associates library content with online learning, and enables librarians to develop stronger connections with instructors and other instructional support staff on campus. In all integration strategies, however, it is important for libraries to keep in mind that campuses may switch learning management systems, so it is best not to be completely dependent on the LMS for reaching out to students. Course level integration can also be time-consuming and have limits to how many courses may be reached. The opportunities and barriers to LMS integration, as well as the rewards and challenges, must be considered as each library strives to support teaching and learning online.

REFERENCES

Bell, Steven J., and John D. Shank. *Academic Librarianship by Design*. Chicago: American Library Association, 2007.

Black, Elizabeth L. "A Toolkit Approach to Integrating Library Resources into the Learning Management System." *Journal of Academic Librarianship* 34, no. 6 (2008): 496–501.

Campus Computing Project. *The 2008 National Survey of Information Technology in U.S. Higher Education Executive Summary*. (2008). http://www.campuscom puting.net/survey (retrieved March 29, 2009).

Casden, Jason, Kim Duckett, Tito Sierra and Joseph Ryan. "Course Views: A Scalable Approach to Providing Course-Based Access to Library Resources." *The Code4Lib Journal*, no. 6 (2009). http://journal.code4lib.org/articles/1218 (retrieved March 31, 2009).

Cohen, David. "Course-Management Software: Where's the Library?" *EDUCAUSE Review* 37, no. 3 (2002): 12–13.

EDUCAUSE Core Data Service. "Faculty and Student Computing," in *EDUCAUSE Core Data Service Fiscal Year 2007 Summary Report*. http://net.educause.edu/apps/coredata/reports/2007 (retrieved March 29, 2009).

Flecker, Dale, and Neil McLean. *Digital Library Content and Course Management Systems: Issues of Interoperability*. Washington, DC: Digital Library Federation, 2004. http://www.diglib.org/pubs/dlf100 (retrieved March 29, 2009).

Gibbons, Susan. "Library Course Management Systems: An Overview." *Library Technology Reports* 41, no. 3 (2005).

Indiana University Digital Library Program. *Sakaibrary: Integrating Licensed Library Resources with Sakai*. http://www.dlib.indiana.edu/projects/sakai/index.shtml (retrieved March 29, 2009).

Jackson, Pamela Alexondra. "Integrating Information Literacy into Blackboard: Building Campus Partnerships for Successful Student Learning." *Journal of Academic Librarianship* 33, no. 4 (2007): 454–61.

Matthew, Victoria, and Ann Schroeder. "The Embedded Librarian Program." *EDUCAUSE Quarterly* 29, no. 4 (2006): 61–65. http://net.educause.edu/ir/library/pdf/EQM06410.pdf (retrieved March 29, 2009).

McLean, Neil, and Clifford Lynch. *Interoperability between Library Information Services and Learning Environments—Bridging the Gap: A Joint White Paper on Behalf of the IMS Global Learning Consortium and the Coalition for Networked Information*. IMS Global Learning Consortium, 2004. http://www.imsproject.org/digitalrepositories/CNIandIMS_2004.pdf (retrieved March 29, 2009).

Rochester Institute of Technology Libraries. "RIT Library's Desire2Learn Integration Project." http://library.rit.edu/desire2learn (retrieved March 29, 2009).

Salaway, Gail, and Judith B. Caruso. *The ECAR Study of Undergraduate Students and Information Technology, 2008* (Research Study, Vol. 8). Boulder, CO: EDUCAUSE Center for Applied Research, 2008. http://www.educause.edu/ecar (retrieved March 29, 2009).

5

AUTHENTICATION AND AUTHORIZATION IN LIBRARIES

David Kennedy

Authentication is the process of verifying and establishing a person's identity. Authorization is the process of enforcing what that person is allowed to do. The authentication process answers the question "Who are you?" The authorization process answers the question "What are you allowed to do?" In everyday life, these two processes are often experienced as one action. A person presents a bank card and four-digit PIN at the ATM machine and is allowed to withdraw from a checking account. Or a person enters in a username and password to retrieve e-mail. From the user perspective, the distinction between authentication and authorization is subtle, and probably not important. The user provides some credentials and is allowed to perform some function.

In the underlying software, though, the distinction is important. In the bank card example, the ATM machine must first authenticate the bank customer. In the authentication process, the ATM verifies the customer's identity with the supplied user credentials: the customer's bank card and the customer's personal PIN. The result of the authentication process is that the ATM machine understands who the individual customer is. In the authorization process, the ATM machine determines which bank accounts the customer is allowed to interact with and withdraw money from. The process is very similar when a user checks e-mail. The e-mail system verifies the user's identity with the supplied user credentials, in this case, a username and password, and uses these credentials to identify a user record in the e-mail system. Then, in the authorization process, the e-mail system determines which e-mail accounts the user has access to.

The processes of authentication and authorization are present in library software as well. For instance, an integrated library system requires a patron to log into the web OPAC in order to place a hold request. A library's interlibrary loan system must understand a patron's institutional affiliation (i.e., faculty, staff, student) when determining whether or not to fulfill a loan request. A third-party electronic resource vendor needs to decide whether or not to allow a user to access the full text of an article. These are all examples of authentication and authorization at work in the library.

It is important for the everyday librarian to understand the basic principles of authentication and authorization. There are key challenges facing libraries and higher education with regards to authentication and authorization, and librarians are going to be involved in determining and implementing solutions to those challenges. One of the challenges is the protection of our patrons' privacy. Another is providing a single sign-on across all library systems to provide a seamless experience for library patrons. Another challenge is to extend a single sign-on environment to integrate with other services on campus, such as learning management software or course home pages. Another key challenge is to facilitate research by providing library users with access to licensed online resources.

This chapter provides an overview of some of the key relevant concepts of authentication and authorization and how they relate to the challenges facing libraries, and introduces some of the technologies and tools that are involved. I will start by introducing some of the key concepts, then discuss how they are applied to a library setting, and then delve deeper into a selection of the technologies that are in use today, namely LDAP, EZproxy, and Shibboleth.

AUTHENTICATION AND AUTHORIZATION CONCEPTS

Authentication

As stated before, authentication is the process which answers the question "Who are you?" The authentication process can be broken down into two steps: user identification and attribute assertion.

In the user identification step, users present some credentials to prove who they are. This step is sometimes referred to as "logging in" or "signing on." Some examples of user credentials are a username/password combination, a thumbprint, a retinal scan, or a hardware device such as a smart card or barcode. The identification process uses the user-supplied credentials to locate a unique identity record and verify that the user is who he says he is.

In some systems, where there is a need for additional security, the user identification step will be a two-factor (or n-factor) authentication process. A two-factor authentication process requires that a user provide more than one set of user credentials. Some examples of two-factor authentication are prompting a user for username and password, then prompting the user with challenge-response questions, and requiring the presence of a smart card as well as a user's PIN.

Once the user's identity is established in the user identification step, the next step is attribute assertion. Attribute assertion is when the authentication process provides information or attributes about the user so that authorization decisions can be made based on those user attributes. In an academic setting, these attributes could include the user's name, contact information, institutional affiliation, and a unique campus identifier. These attributes may even include a user's registered course list.

Authorization

Authorization is the process which answers the question "What are you allowed to do?" Based on a combination of user attributes and an arbitrary set of criteria, an application determines what actions a user is allowed to perform. Authorization policies are typically determined by the application that is providing services to the user.

Single Sign-On

Traditionally, software systems that require user accounts have handled authentication and authorization internally. They have provided web interfaces that allow individuals to log in to perform functions. However, with authentication and authorization handled internally to each application, a user needs to log into each application separately.

Single sign-on is a property of multiple independent software systems, by which a user logs in once and is able to access the multiple systems without having to log in again. In a single sign-on environment, the authentication process is decoupled from the system where the user will be performing their tasks. Because a single sign-on system interacts with multiple software systems, it is inherently separate from the systems that it provides authentication for. And those systems that use single sign-on must rely on external means of authentication.

In every single sign-on scenario, some level of trust must be established between the single sign-on system and the software systems that it provides authentication for. Each single sign-on system may handle establishing the trust relationship in different ways, such as cookies or sharing of SSL certificates. The important concept to note is that the single sign-on system is asserting the identity of the user to the software system. In order for the software system to accept the assertion, some trust relationship must be established so that the software system can rely on the validity of the assertion from the single sign-on system.

Identity Management

Identity management deals with the life cycle and management of a user's identity information in an organization. Within an organization, there are often many software systems that require some identity information about the individuals who will be using the systems. Identity management involves the creation and deletion of user information that will be used by these systems, as well as synchronization of this information across all software systems within the organization. A key component of identity management is a single sign-on among software systems within the organization.

In a university setting, there are several software systems requiring identity information. The bursar, human resources, financial, student information systems, and libraries are all examples of systems on a university campus that require information about users' identities. Often, universities centralize identity information and present a single directory for all users affiliated with the university. LDAP (Lightweight Directory Access Protocol) is the prevailing protocol for providing a directory.

The processes of synchronizing identity data between systems is called provisioning and deprovisioning of data. Provisioning of identity data is a central identity management service that sends identity information updates to all systems requiring notification of changes. Deprovisioning of identity data is a central identity management service that sends delete notifications when a user has been deleted. In an academic setting, integrated library systems maintain patron databases. In some cases, these patron databases are kept current by the provisioning/deprovisioning process. There is a defined standard, SPML (Service Provisioning Markup Language), for the transmission of these provisioning and deprovisioning messages on a real-time basis, although it is not clear how widely adopted these are among integrated library systems. The majority of integrated library systems are still updated periodically in batch mode.

Federated Identity Management

Federated identity management is single sign-on extended beyond organizational boundaries. In federated identity management, users are allowed access to services based on assertions made by another known and trusted organization that the identity of the user has been verified. Just as in single sign-on systems discussed above, the trust relationships between organizations are extremely important in making a federated identity management framework function.

CHALLENGES FACING LIBRARIES

Patron Privacy

In a university setting, libraries are faced with the challenge of providing personalized service to their constituencies while protecting their privacy.

At the university, there are challenges in this regard for both the central IT as well as in the library. Central IT maintains software systems that contain masses of user information about the campus population, information about both students and university employees. In an era of identity theft, the amount of personally identifiable user information is a target ripe for hacking. So, it becomes very important for central IT to take measures to protect that data. To do this, many universities are examining practices and policies, and sometimes changing how they share information, in order to limit the amount of user data that is shared across networks. To some degree, this has had an effect on libraries because library systems may need to adapt to retrieving less user information in the provisioning and deprovisioning processes from central IT. Or the libraries may now need to retrieve this information in more secure ways than they did in the past.

Another way in which campuses need to be mindful of the sharing of user information is when providing authentication for third-party library resources. In order to provide personalized services to users, library resource providers need to identify an individual so that the next time that individual uses their resource, they can identify the individual and retrieve stored information about that user. These third-party resource providers can only identify an individual based on the information that is shared by the university. Federated identity management software provides universities with a mechanism to provide authentication across organizational boundaries and assert user attributes to resource providers as well. One of these in particular, Shibboleth, allows universities to control each user attribute, and which attribute is shared with which resource provider. With Shibboleth, a university may share a user's name and campus affiliation with one resource provider but may choose to share only a persistent opaque identifier (a unique ID that does not include personally identifiable information) with another resource provider. In this way, the university can allow for a resource provider to present its users with personalized service without compromising the user's identity.

Access to Online Resources

Libraries have been facilitating access to licensed resources long before federated identity management solutions were conceived and developed. An early method of access was to provide CD-ROM applications directly to libraries, and the resources were available from certain PCs within the library. Demand outgrew the capacity of this solution, and resource providers started putting their content on the Web. However, because resource providers wanted to control the access to be able to license the use, they needed ways to restrict access to the content. Some of the ways this has been accomplished have been to share widely a username and password, to use Referring URLs, and to use IP authentication. The dissemination of usernames and passwords is self explanatory, and it is easy to see how this solution provided some scalability challenges. Referring URL is a mechanism by which resource providers only grant access to a resource request if that request originated from a known Referring URL. Libraries implemented this by creating links to resources on certain Web pages or programmatically creating the resource request and putting the appropriate Referring URL into the Referrer header of the request. With IP authentication, libraries contract with the resource provider for IP addresses or ranges of IP addresses to be allowed access to the resource. Furthermore, remote access can be provided to patrons with the use of proxy servers or URL rewriting proxies, like EZproxy.

These methods of providing access control to resources work fairly well. However, none of them allow resource providers to provide personalized services to users. There is a solution that does allow resource providers the ability to provide personalized service: federated identity management. With a federated identity management solution, the library or the campus provides authentication and delivers some set of user attributes to the resource provider. The resource provider can then make authorization decisions based on those attributes, as well as retrieve user account information in order to provide personalized service to the user. Shibboleth is an example of a federated identity management solution that can provide this sort of authentication to resource providers.

Integration with Campus Services

In addition to providing authentication for third-party online resources, university libraries also have the challenge of trying to integrate the services that the library provides with other campus services. In most cases, integration equates to a single sign-on, where users can move seamlessly from campus services to library services without needing to authenticate more than once. Some examples of campus services that are most applicable to a single sign-on with the library are a campus portal, learning management systems, and course home pages. Portals provide individualized service to campus members, and it is desirable for libraries to have a presence in the campus portal to allow students to view the status of their loans or ILL requests, and to link to their account pages in the library systems. In learning management systems and course home pages, teachers want to be able to provide links to library resources, and they want these links to be authenticated links, meaning that they will not require additional logins for the student.

Integration with these campus services can be achieved if both the campus services and the library services use the same single sign-on mechanism. There are also ways this can be achieved by implementing federated identity management products, such as Shibboleth, on top of existing single sign-on systems. Shibboleth was designed with a modular architecture, which allows for using a pluggable single sign-on system as a part of its architecture. By implementing Shibboleth on top of an existing single sign-on system, services that are Shibboleth-enabled can have a single sign-on with those services that are already using the existing single sign-on system. By way of an example, let's say that a library wants a single sign-on between a Blackboard learning management system and the library's course reserves system; doing so would allow a professor to place links on course pages in Blackboard to reserve material for the course. Let's also assume that the Blackboard system uses the campus's CAS (Central Authentication Service) for authentication and single sign-on, and also assume that the course reserves system is Shibboleth-enabled, but not necessarily CAS-enabled. A Shibboleth identity provider could be installed, using CAS for the single sign-on piece, in order to provide the single sign-on between Blackboard and the course reserves system.

KEY TECHNOLOGIES

There are many technologies and software solutions that are relevant to discussions of authentication and authorization. I won't discuss them all here but will discuss a few of the technologies and protocols that I have found to be particularly useful in meeting the authentication challenges facing libraries.

LDAP

LDAP stands for Lightweight Directory Access Protocol. LDAP is a popular standard protocol for providing directory services at universities. The protocol includes a handful of operations for managing, searching, and authenticating against a directory. A directory contains entries, each entry usually representing a person. The search operation is used to search and read entries. The bind operation is used to verify user credentials. There are also operations for adding, modifying, and deleting entries. The operations of most interest in the context of authentication and authorization are search and bind. Bind allows systems to use LDAP to perform credential verification. Search allows systems to query the directory and ascertain user attributes from the directory entries. Hence, LDAP has become the plumbing for authentication and authorization.

Most library applications requiring some means of authentication are capable of using the LDAP protocol to access an authoritative source of user information to serve its authentication needs. Also, most single sign-on solutions, as well as federated identity management products, are capable of using LDAP.

EZproxy

EZproxy is a URL rewriting proxy developed by Chris Zagar. It is widely used by libraries to provide access to online resources. URL rewriting proxies perform the same function as traditional proxy servers, in that they act as a go-between for requests from the browser to the web resource. In both types of proxy servers, the requests appear to originate from the IP of the proxy server. The difference is that traditional proxies require that the user configure their browsers to use the proxy server whereas users don't need to make any browser configurations to use URL rewriting proxies. The URL rewriting proxy server changes the URLs in the Web pages that it is proxying so that subsequent requests are routed back through the proxy server.

EZproxy provides access control to licensed resources. The resources need only be configured with IP address ranges that include the IP address of the EZproxy server.

So, EZproxy provides a means for authenticated sessions to licensed resources. It also provides a simple way to create authenticated URLs to the licensed resource; the process of creating the authenticated URL is simply to take the original resource's URL, and prepend the address of the EZproxy server to it. For example, to authenticate a link to http://www.resource. com/resource, Example University could create the following URL: http:// ezproxy.example.edu/login?url=http://www.resource.com/resource. As the example illustrates, it is very easy to generate these authenticated links. This ease of use allows for integration into static web pages. Also, most library software that generates dynamic links to resources is capable of being configured to generate these links as EZproxy-authenticated URLs.

EZproxy is also adaptable to a myriad of authentication schemes. There are a handful of out-of-the-box supported authentication options, as well as the ability to write your own authentication module or redirect to an external web service or CGI script that provides authentication. Furthermore, EZproxy is capable of consuming user attributes from some authentication mechanisms and making authorization decisions based on user attributes. The way in which this typically works is that users get assigned into configured EZproxy groups, based on the user's attributes, such as institutional affiliation. EZproxy databases (i.e., resources) are also configured with groups, and users are only allowed access to the databases that match their group assignment.

Shibboleth

Shibboleth is an open source federated identity management software developed by Internet2. Shibboleth provides single sign-on and authentication services within an organization and across organizational boundaries. The Shibboleth software is modular and consists of two main entities, an identity provider and a service provider. The identity provider includes the functions of user identification and attribute assertion. The service provider is integrated into the web server where the resources reside and provides user attributes to the resource in order for it to make authorization decisions.

The Shibboleth architecture relies on established trust relationships between identity providers and service providers. In order to facilitate the communication between servers during the authentication process, Shibboleth uses the SAML (Security Assertion Markup Language) protocol to encapsulate attribute assertions from the identity provider to the service provider. Before this form of communication can begin, both identity provider and service provider need to be configured to trust each other. This is done by configuring each entity with metadata about the other entities they will be interacting with. This metadata includes location and support information for each entity, as well as SSL information, such as certificates, in order to verify the authenticity of the entities they interact with.

Trust relationship metadata is also collected by federations. Federations are groups of identity providers and service providers that see value in interoperating. The collection of metadata by federations eases the process of metadata configuration because there are fewer places to go in order to collect the metadata. All federation members publish or register their metadata to the federation, where it is dispersed to all other federation members.

In addition to trust relationships, there is another main point of configuration that details the interactions between the identity and service providers. This area has to do with attribute assertion—which user attributes are shared by the identity provider to which service provider(s). This configuration is done in the attribute release policies of the identity provider. I won't detail the configuration, but, in brief, the attribute release policies are XML structures that define the attributes to release and how they are identified, and which service providers to share which attributes with.

Like EZproxy, the Shibboleth identity provider software was designed to work with a myriad of single sign-on mechanisms, and also to work with a variety of stores of user data. Single sign-on mechanisms can range from a flat file or a database backend to an enterprise single sign-on software like CAS. Likewise, Shibboleth can be configured to retrieve user attributes from different sources, such as an LDAP server.

On the service provider side, there are configurations for what attributes to request from the identity provider(s) and also how to name those attributes when delivering them to the resource. In the service provider implementation, the service provider is integrated into the web server and processes each HTTP request for the underlying service, adding the attributes to the HTTP request. It does this by setting HTTP headers for the attributes. The aforementioned attribute configurations instruct the service provider how it should name the HTTP headers that it uses to deliver the user attributes to the resource.

The Shibboleth technology has allowed for a single sign-on across library applications, single sign-on between library applications and campus applications, and for extending the single sign-on environment beyond the campus to resource providers.

EZproxy and Shibboleth

The combination of EZproxy and Shibboleth allows for some opportunities for libraries to solve a lot of the authentication challenges that they are currently faced with. EZproxy allows for ease of use of creating authenticated URLs. EZproxy is integrated into existing library applications that create dynamic links to content. Shibboleth can provide a true single sign-on across a wide range of applications, both inside and outside of a campus's domain. Shibboleth can release user attributes to service providers in a controlled and secure manner to allow service providers to make their own authorization decisions. All of these advantages can be brought together to provide a single sign-on to licensed resources and allow those resources to personalize their interfaces for the individual while protecting the individual's privacy. In addition, Shibboleth and EZproxy can be combined to provide attribute-based authorization to licensed resources.

There are two main pieces to the integration of EZproxy and Shibboleth. The first is to configure EZproxy as a Shibboleth service provider. The second is to configure EZproxy database configurations as Shibboleth databases.

The EZproxy documentation provides sufficient documentation on how to configure EZproxy as a service provider, so I won't dwell on the details. But, I will explain the reasons for configuring EZproxy as a service provider. The most obvious reason is to have single sign-on with EZproxy. Just as important, though, is that EZproxy, as a Shibboleth service provider, is capable of consuming user attributes provided by the Shibboleth identity provider, and can make authorization decisions based on those attributes. This is done by configuring rules in the shib.usr file that associate Shibboleth attributes with EZproxy groups, and then assigning database configurations to EZproxy groups. In this way, users are restricted to those databases for which they have the appropriate user attributes.

The second piece to integration of EZproxy and Shibboleth is to configure EZproxy database configurations as Shibboleth databases. This involves the use of SPUEdit commands in EZproxy and resource providers implementing Shibboleth SessionInitiators. In EZproxy, SPU stands for Starting Point URL. SPUEdit commands can be cleverly placed in the EZproxy configuration to redirect URLs for a particular resource through that resource's SessionInitiator. The Shibboleth SessionInitiator is a URL within the Shibboleth Service Provider that acts as a Shibboleth session initiator and is capable of establishing the session with the correct identity provider seamlessly.

With EZproxy and the Shibboleth service provider configured correctly, it is possible for users to navigate seamlessly to a variety of resources and be able to take advantage of their personalization features.

CONCLUSION

There are more authentication and authorization technologies in addition to the ones that I have highlighted. And there are more complex authentication challenges that are looming, especially as library licensed resources become discoverable in contexts outside of the library domain, such as by search engines. My intent with this chapter was to give an overview of the relevant concepts and library challenges, as well as describe some of the technologies that I think are important building blocks to meeting current and future challenges, so that the everyday librarian is more equipped to face them.

6

CONTENT MANAGEMENT SYSTEMS

Frances Rice

Have you ever found out-of-date information displayed on Web sites, like events that occurred several months ago? Alternatively, have you noticed an inconsistent look and feel among pages of a site, such as pages having different headers or footers? Do you need to update content on your site but find it challenging because the content is scattered among several pages throughout your site? Are you in charge of keeping content on the site up-to-date but do not have access to the web server? On the other hand, is it your responsibility to complete every change to content on your site, and you are overwhelmed with the number of changes? If you find yourself agreeing to one or more of these questions, you've seen examples of problems that a web Content Management System (CMS) is designed to solve.

This chapter will provide the nontechnical librarian with a basic understanding of a web CMS. There is a brief history on Web site management, and the concept of content being created and stored outside of Web site design is introduced. It presents basic information on how a CMS works. In addition, there is a section that describes where you can find information on CMS vendors and offers some guidelines on choosing a CMS. The chapter ends with a discussion on three different CMS options: home-grown, commercial vendors, and open source software.

A web content management system is a process for managing the content of your Web site (Rawlins 2004). This could be as simple as submitting all revisions and additions to one person on your staff. It could be a web-editing procedure developed in-house, or it could be a commercial product. Regardless of the process and however you manage a Web site, you already have a

CMS. A question that needs to be addressed is whether the CMS is the appropriate one for your needs.

Content management systems are not a product of the World Wide Web. They were first used by large publishing companies that needed a system to track production of their print projects. Publishers tracked prepublications through creation and review to final publication. With the development of the Web, publishers wanted to take advantage of the new technology and adapted their CMS to the new format (Rawlins 2004).

BACKGROUND

Understanding the CMS concept requires some background information on Web site creation. During the early years of Web site construction, pages were created using HTML or by using web authoring tools such as Dreamweaver or FrontPage. These tools combined the content with the presentation all in one document. Tags of HTML code contained formatting information for the document. Library hours on a web page might be coded like this:

<font face = "comic sans serif"size = "3"> The library will close at 5:00 pm. </font>

and would appear on the site looking like this:

The library will close at 5:00 pm.

An advantage to using web authoring tools like Dreamweaver or Frontpage is that web pages can be created quickly with minimal knowledge of HTML. Any web browser can interpret the HTML code and display the content according to that code.

A disadvantage of these tools is that every new web page needs to have formatting information included by either hand coding HTML or cutting and pasting code from a preexisting page. Room for error increases the potential for inconsistent formatting among pages as more and more pages are added to the Web site. Processes were developed to alleviate errors. One example keeps the management of the site under one person's control in an attempt to standardize the code. Another method publishes web pages to a test server for review before posting to the live Web site.

A better method of Web site management is separation of content from style. This allows the look and feel of a Web site to be stored in one document, while content is stored in another. Dave Clark maintains that the separation of content from presentation is fundamental to content management. Clark (2008) further explains why content and presentation need to be divided: "Content is a thing to be created, stored, and managed, and presentation is a thing to be added just in time for the content to appear in a form suitable for human use" (40).

Although usually overlooked, the method for managing a Web site needs to be considered during its construction. The type of CMS selected drives how content is created and stored. One simple process for content management is to use a Cascading Style Sheet (CSS) to store most of the style and formatting for the site, and write the individual pages using PHP, a web scripting language. A line of CSS might look like:

```
hours {font-family: Comic Sans Serif;
font-size: 12pt;
font-weight: bold;
font-style: italic;
font-variant: small-caps;}
```

This defines how a portion of content that has been tagged as "hours" will be displayed.

A corresponding PHP document would use the CSS information in its script as:

```
<div class = "hours">The library will close at 5:00 pm.</div>
```

Combining the information about the formatting for "hours" in the CSS with the PHP code, a web browser would display the code as:

The library will close at 5:00 pm.

From this point forward the only information needing to be changed is the phrase "The library will close at 5:00 pm." The look or presentation remains constant.

CSS and PHP represent an important shift from static HTML pages (pages with information that does not change frequently) to dynamically driven content and the concept of separating content from style (Dahl 2004). Instead of building Web sites from many stand-alone pages found in multiple files and directories, content is stored in a database that is combined with a template file and displayed on sites at the point of need (Austin 2008). When a user encounters a site using PHP, it looks like a site using HTML. However, when a browser encounters a site using PHP files, it interprets the PHP code stored within the files. The code retrieves the associated content stored in a database, combines it with the CSS, and renders the page on the fly.

HOW DOES A CMS WORK?

A CMS is like a large repository that houses all content outside of the Web site. Within the repository, information is divided into logical elements and saved. These logical elements have been labeled or tagged and can be effectively retrieved by a piece of code, combined with a style template, and displayed as a single web page on a Web site (Rockley 2003, 312). See figure 6.1.

When style is separate from content, it can be reused with multiple styles and formats. Instead of retyping the same content on multiple pages, it is entered once, tagged, and stored for future use. For example, a description for the database LexisNexis Academic-Business can appear in three different web locations: the OPAC, in a listing of databases, and on a course-specific web page. The idea is to have each location display slightly different information about the database as needed by a user (see table 6.1).

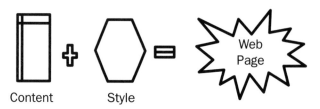

Content   Style   Web Page

Figure 6.1. Separation of Content from Style.

Table 6.1.

Database description in OPAC	Database description page	Database description in course guide
Provides full text business articles from newspapers, magazines, journals, wires and transcripts. Also includes industry news, accounting journals & literature and company information.	LexisNexis Academic-Business is a collection of databases specifically tailored for universities. Almost all of the 5,000 publications on Lexis-Nexis Universe are available in full text. The service covers newspapers, magazines, wire services, federal and state court opinions, federal and state statutes, federal regulations, and SEC filings such as 10-Ks, 10-Qs, and their exhibits. News information is updated daily and wire services several times daily.	Includes reports from Hoover's, plus corporate family trees, and links to full-text news items, financial, intellectual property, and legal case information.

The information is combined into one unified description for the database and stored for future use:

> LexisNexis Academic-Business is a collection of databases that provides full-text business articles from newspapers, magazines, wire services, and transcripts. It contains industry news, accounting journals & literature, and company information. You can search for financial, intellectual property, and legal case information. Reports from Hoover's and corporate family trees are included.

As various uses for the content are identified, the unified description is tagged to indicate which components are appropriate for each section of a site:

> <LexisNexis Academic—Business is a collection of databases that provides full-text business articles from newspapers, magazines, wire services, and transcripts.> [*OPAC, database listing, course guide*] <It contains industry news, accounting journals & literature, and company information.> [*database listing, course guide*] <You can search for financial, intellectual property, and legal case information. Reports from Hoover's and corporate family trees are included.> [*course guide*]

Table 6.2.

Database description in OPAC	Database description page	Database description in course guide
LexisNexis Academic-Business is a collection of databases that provides full-text business, articles from newspapers, magazines, wire services, and transcripts.	LexisNexis Academic-Business is a collection of databases that provides full-text business articles from newspapers, magazines, wire services, and transcripts.	LexisNexis Academic-Business is a collection of databases that provides full-text business articles from newspapers, magazines, wire services, and transcripts.
	It contains industry news, accounting journals & literature, and company information.	It contains industry news, accounting journals & literature, and company information.
		You can search for financial, intellectual property, and legal case information. Reports from Hoover's and corporate family trees are included.

The unified description now includes a brief descriptive sentence (the first line) that can be used in the OPAC, the database description page, and the course guide. The second sentence includes additional descriptive information for the database description page. Finally, all sections are included with the Course Description information to provide users with information and terminology specific and helpful for their course work.

Using the same unified description on multiple pages provides for consistent information throughout the site. When content is stored as discrete elements, updates can be made quickly. Chunking information also provides the ability to use content from a CMS in other applications that can interpret the partitioned data (Austin 2008). A Rich Site Summary (RSS) feed is one example of how the chunked information can be interpreted by another application. Users sign up for an RSS feed from their favorite Web sites to alert them when new information has been posted. The tagged information in the CMS can be interpreted by the RSS feed to deliver up-to-date information to users without someone manually retrieving information and integrating it with the RSS. Users can retrieve RSS feeds from their computers, cell phones, or other handheld devices.

A CMS provides the ability to assign different levels of access, maintaining site security. A supervisor can publish updated policies and procedures directly to departmental pages while another staff member can write content that has to be approved before it is displayed. The CMS also allows staff members to update pages on the Web site with little knowledge of HTML or the need for web authoring tools.

Because a CMS reduces the need for advanced HTML training, sections of a Web site can be assigned to multiple people for maintenance. Expanding maintenance responsibilities from one staff member to many staff members reduces the potential backlog of maintenance issues. This can also reduce turnaround time for completing modifications, which in turn keeps Web sites up-to-date and current.

A CMS provides the ability to store multiple versions. This feature allows edits to be tracked. If a mistake is made or if something is published accidentally, it is very easy to roll back to a previous version. Also, if a site is migrated to a different CMS, the content can easily be imported to the new system.

CHOOSING A CMS

Libraries have two types of information to manage, vendor-supplied and local. Locally created material has more flexibility in presentation and content. Vendor-supplied resources, like an online catalog, database, or digital repository, contain a built-in CMS. Libraries do not have complete control of the display. Instead, presentation is determined through the selection of a template. To help libraries choose among vendors, Wisniewski and Stenström (2007) assembled a table listing the top 10 vendors that offer aggregated content management. These systems can integrate disparate databases and content into one unified index that can be searched by users seamlessly. The authors compiled the table based on two criteria. The first was the vendor's ability to integrate with existing systems, like an ILS (Integrated Library System) or a database supplier. The second was whether the system could be used out of the box, or if it needed additional time and resources for configuration and implementation.

Besides vendor-supplied content, libraries have locally developed content that needs to be managed: policies, hours, services, or staff directories. With about 2,000 available CMS vendors, choosing the right system to manage this content can be difficult. Andy Austin suggests there are three common attributes found in all CMS products:

- They provide a framework for creating, managing, and publishing web-based content.
- They provide a secure environment with managed user roles.
- They provide extensions for enhanced capabilities. (Austin 2008)

In addition to the common features of editing, security, and enhanced capabilities, Bob Doyle (2007) recommends creating a list of the content and services that are currently provided by your library's site, plus additional content and new features you want to add. He suggests that the list should align with identifiable goals in an organization's mission and strategic plan. By using this list, it becomes easier to determine which CMS supports your needs, how well, and at what cost.

The CMS Report (http://cmsreport.com/category/cms-made-simple) was launched to highlight the latest developments in the world of content management systems, like the release of new CMS systems. The site also offers online articles, blog postings, and other content written by Bryan Ruby, the host and author of the site. The site's main focus is on the latest information in the CMS area, and it provides links to reviews of open source and commercial CMS systems.

The Web CMS Report, from CMS Watch, (http://www.cmswatch.com/About/) offers a comprehensive overview of web content management products and best practices. It includes comparative surveys of the top-40 CMS packages that include enterprise systems, mid-market, and open source. The reports are downloadable and average between $1,000 and $2,000 per report, a prohibitive cost for smaller libraries.

Quoin, Inc., a software development company that helps in selecting, planning, building, and installing a CMS, has supplied an extensive table of CMS requirements. The table is organized by various user functions, like administrators or authors, and then by features that address design and implementation, authentication and authorization, and the acquisition of content from outside sources. The complete table of functionality and recommended

Table 6.3.

Feature	Examples
System requirements	Operating system, approximate costs
Security	Audit trails, content approval, types of authentication supported
Support	Manuals, certification program offered, professional services
Ease of use	Drag and drop content, Image resizing, Spell checker
Management	Asset management, Content staging, themes
Interoperability	RSS, FTP support
Flexibility	Multisite deployment, Content reuse,
Built-in application	Blog, Chat, Wiki

features can be viewed at (http://www.quoininc.com/quoin/content-man agement-systems/wcms-requirements.html).

The CMS Matrix (http://cmsmatrix.org) lists over 1,000 products, open-source and commercial. This service allows users to compare CMS products on a variety of features (see table 6.3).

The listing for products is submitted and maintained by expert users or by the manufacturer. The site includes links to other CMS resources, a FAQ section, and a discussion section where people can post questions (Kneale 2008).

Besides the functionality of a CMS, there are other important factors that need to be considered. These include installation costs and annual maintenance fees. In addition, support costs, including staff salaries and hardware maintenance, are factors that are above and beyond the purchase price of a CMS. Depending on the size of the site and the number of staff needed to support the CMS, these yearly costs may outweigh the initial costs of a CMS. These last considerations might influence the type of CMS chosen, that is, commercial product, open source software, or a locally developed system.

WHO USES A CMS?

A survey conducted in 2006 asked 110 academic-library web developers if they used a CMS. About one in four answered yes. The survey revealed that the use of a CMS was dependent on the size of the library. Surprisingly, larger libraries did not use a CMS as much as the smaller libraries. Larger libraries reported having staff with sufficient web design knowledge enabling them to manage complex Web sites without the use of a CMS. On the other hand, smaller libraries reported not having knowledgeable web designers on staff and used a CMS to build and maintain their sites. The survey concluded that smaller libraries were more likely to use a CMS than larger institutions (Connell 2008).

CMS VENDORS

In 2007, the University of California, Davis, conducted a survey to determine CMS use among colleges and universities in the United States. Out of 129 responses received, 62 percent (81) answered that their institution used a CMS. Of those 81 institutions, 18 used a custom built or homegrown CMS. The rest used either open source or commercial solutions. Four products most frequently reported by participants were open source (see table 6.4).

Additional information collected during the survey revealed that the average price for a CMS was $49,140 for software and licensing plus an additional $14,954 for hardware. It also reported the breakdown on campus-wide implementations, departmental implementations, and the use of multiple CMSs across the campus. The survey found that the average number of staff used for implementation was between one and five members. Support was reported to be provided by a centralized staff, using one to three staff members. When asked what advice they would give to universities looking for a CMS, respondents' answers had some common threads. Their advice included setting realistic timelines, knowing what you want to get out of using a CMS, making up a requirement list, and getting buy-in from all areas impacted by a CMS. Open source was also suggested by universities and colleges as an alternative to purchasing a commercial product, citing the ability to download and test prior to implementation, and the ability to adapt the system to meet local needs. On the downside, one participant recognized that open source does not mean free; there are development and support costs. The complete survey can be found at http://cms.ucdavis.edu/cms survey/index.php.

Table 6.4.

Product	Web site
Plone	http://plone.org/
Drupal	http://drupal.org/
ZOPE Content Management Framework	http://www.zope.org/
Joomla!	http://www.joomla.org/

CUSTOM-BUILT CMS

A custom built or homegrown CMS solution offers many, but not all of the advantages of a commercial CMS. These custom solutions can provide the ability to simplify and distribute content administration. They can also simplify the creation of content by providing a web-based form to contributors. The contributors fill in the information in the appropriate boxes on the form and submit it via the Web. A homegrown CMS can include a centralized graphic design by providing design templates and database-driven content storage.

Gonzaga University in Spokane, Washington, had a homegrown CMS but eventually migrated to a commercial product. They wanted automated workflow management, which ensures that the correct approval processes are followed, and they wanted to be able to reuse content, allowing for consistency of information throughout their site. Being able to track revisions and document the various versions of their site was important. Their homegrown system was lacking in key areas. There was no access control process and no ability to assign different security roles. Their system could not connect with other systems across campus. This resulted in some information, like special programming, being maintained in multiple databases across their campus instead of one central database. Gonzaga wanted to move to a campus-wide implementation, but their old system was not robust enough to expand to support all campus Web sites. Finally, their system required significant resources to maintain and even greater resources to improve and extend functionality (Powell 2003).

COMMERCIAL CMS

Purchasing a commercial CMS might be a solution for libraries that do not have the staff to create their own. There are advantages to using a commercial CMS. You do not need staff to create templates; you simply select one. You are not responsible for training staff how to use the CMS; the vendor conducts training. Vendors have experience with CMS implementation and can draw on that experience during subsequent installations. They will guide and provide support to their clients throughout setup.

On the downside, you are limited to the functionality built into the system. A commercial CMS solution may be too costly. Many CMS solutions offer campus-wide solutions and have many more features than are necessary in a library environment. In addition to start-up costs, there are annual maintenance and licensing fees.

Vendors that offer an enterprise CMS solution are listed in table 6.5.

An alternative to purchasing a commercial CMS solution is an out-of-the-box application like Adobe Contribute (http://www.adobe.com/products/contribute/) or Ektron CMS400.net (http://www.ektron.com/cms/). These

Table 6.5.

Hannon Hill Cascade Server	http://www.hannonhill.com/products/cascade-server/index.html
Ingeniux	http://www.ingeniux.com/
Interwoven Teamsite	http://www.interwoven.com/components/pagenext.jsp?topic=PRODUCT::TEAMSITE
OmniUpdate	http://omniupdate.com/
PaperThin Commonspot	http://www.paperthin.com/
RedDot (Open Text) CMS	http://www.reddot.com/services.htm
Sitecore	http://www.sitecore.net/
Vignette	http://www.vignette.com/

products are geared towards smaller Web sites and may be more appealing because of their lower purchase price. However, these applications do not provide the same level of installation support, nor do they assist with setup, implementation, or training.

OPEN SOURCE

A solution that is growing in popularity is open source. By definition, open source is a program that is distributed with the source code, a collection of programming statements. These statements allow programmers to communicate with computers and tell them what to do. With access to the source code, subsequent programmers can tailor the code to meet their requirements. In addition to customization, open source software is freely available for download via the Web.

Open source blogging software, like WordPress (http://wordpress.org), has been a popular alternative to commercial products. Briefly, "blogging" is similar to an online journal or diary that is regularly updated and allows others to leave comments. Libraries have used blogs to keep their patrons up-to-date with what's new at the library, to share knowledge, and to solicit feedback. Because WordPress allows for the creation and management of blog posts and static pages, some libraries have expanded its use to include a CMS. Libraries use it to post timely content, like special programming or events, and permanent content, like services and staff (Farkas 2008 "Our New").

WordPress offers many predefined templates that allow libraries to develop a site that does not resemble a blog. Libraries can also create their own templates by making changes to the CSS. Troy Public Library in New York (http://thetroylibrary.org) and Lamson Library and Learning Commons in

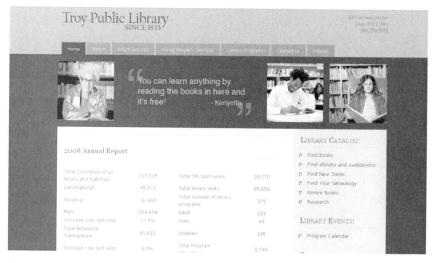

Figure 6.2. Site Using WordPress.

Designed by chardeconsulting.com.

New Hampshire (http://library.plymouth.edu/) are examples of Web sites developed using WordPress (see figure 6.2).

Wikis are an example of another open source software that has been used as a CMS, like PmWiki (http://pmwiki.org), MediaWiki (http://me diawiki.org), and TikiWiki (tikiwiki.org). Wikis have features similar to a CMS, allowing multiple users to create, modify, and organize web page content. Unlike a typical wiki, which allows for collaboration by many users, these wikis are only open for staff to edit. They can be styled to look like any other Web site by editing the CSS (Cascading Style Sheet). Wikis are very useful to libraries that want to allow multiple staff members to maintain the content of their Web site. The University of South Carolina in Aiken (http://library.usca.edu/) is an example of PmWiki, and Douglas County Library System of Oregon (http://www.dclibrary.us/tiki-index.php) used TikiWiki to develop their site. Florida State University Libraries (http://www.lib.fsu.edu/help/researchguides) used MediaWiki for their research guides (Farkas 2008 "Wiki Way"). All of these wikis provide the same Web site feel. Choosing one over the other is a personal preference (see figure 6.3).

Drupal (http://drupal.org) is a popular open source CMS that allows libraries to manage web content easily and have both static and dynamic features on their site. With Drupal, it is not necessary to maintain separate systems, like a wiki or a blog, from the main Web site. These can be integrated using one of the hundreds of Drupal modules or add-ons (Farkas 2008 "Next Gen").

One Drupal module, SOPAC 2.0, integrates the OPAC with a library's Web site. This provides the opportunity for patrons to write reviews of materials

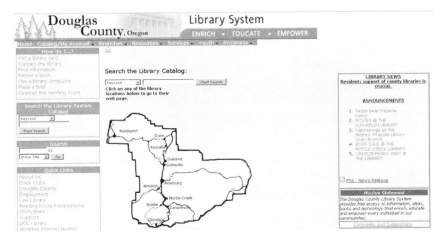

Figure 6.3. Site Using TikiWiki.

Douglas County (OR) Library System.

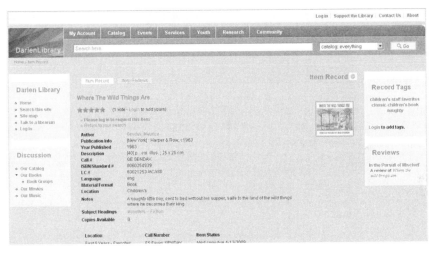

Figure 6.4. Site Using Drupal and SOPAC 2.0.

Darien Library.

that are listed in the catalog. It also enables them to rate materials. The Darien Public Library in Connecticut (http://www.darienlibrary.org/catalog) is an example of a library using Drupal and SOPAC 2.0 with their ILS, Innovative Interfaces (Sheehan 2009). Other libraries cited by Sheehan include Ann Arbor, Michigan District Library (http://aadl.org) and the Stowe Free Library in Vermont (http://stowelibrary.org). See figure 6.4.

There are drawbacks to using open source software. One difficulty is the reliance on in-house developers to install and maintain the software. This dependence may prove challenging if the developer leaves the employment of the library. Unlike a commercial CMS with its team of developers, the library becomes responsible for locating and hiring a replacement. In addition, support may be difficult to find. There is no formal customer support but rather a community of users that volunteer support.

SUMMARY

Web content management systems are finding their way into libraries. There are over 1,000 vendors from which to choose. In addition to commercial products, libraries use homegrown systems successfully. Also, open source software that was developed for one purpose, like blogging or wikis, has been employed as an alternative to customary CMS solutions. The Web sites managed with commercial products, open source software, or homegrown solutions all look the same to end users. It doesn't matter which one you choose; using a CMS makes the management of a Web site easier.

REFERENCES

Austin, Andy and Christopher Harris. "Welcome to a New Paradigm." *Library Technology Reports* 44, no. 4 (2008): 5–7.

Clark, Dave. "Content Management and the Separation of Presentation and Content." *Technical Communication Quarterly* 17, no. 1 (2008): 35–60.

Connell, Ruth Sara. "Survey of Web Developers in Academic Libraries." *Journal of Academic Librarianship* 34, no. 2 (March 2008): 121–29.

Dahl, Mark. "Content Management Strategy for a College Library Web Site." *Information Technology & Libraries* 23, no. 1 (March 2004): 23–29.

Doyle, Bob. "Compare and Contrast CMS." *EContent* 30, no. 1 (January/February 2007): 31.

Farkas, Meredith. "CMS for Next-Gen Websites." *American Libraries* 39, no. 10 (November 2008): 36.

Farkas, Meredith. "CMS the Wiki Way." *American Libraries* 39, no. 11 (December 2008): 35.

Farkas, Meredith. "Our New Website is a Blog." *American Libraries* 39, no. 9 (October 2008): 45.

Kneale, Ruth. "From Static to Dynamic." *Computers in Libraries* 28, no. 3 (March 2008): 16–20.

Powell, Wayne and Chris Gill. "Web Content Management Systems in Higher Education." *Educause Quarterly* 26, no. 2 (2003): 43–50.

Rawlins, Nathan. *Web Content Management for Dummies.* Indianapolis, Ind.: Wiley Pub, 2004.

Rockley, Ann, Pamela Kostur, and Steve Manning. *Managing Enterprise Content.* Indianapolis, Ind.: New Riders, 2003.

Sheehan, Kate. "Creating Open Source Conversation." *Computers in Libraries* 29, no. 2 (February 2009): 8–11.

Wisniewski, Jeff, and Cheryl Stenström. "Content Management Systems." *Computers in Libraries* 27, no. 2 (February 2007): 17–22.

7

DATA VISUALIZATION

Steve McCann

What we're dealing with now isn't information overload [...] it really is a filtering problem rather than an information [problem].
—Clay Shirky (2008)

My first introduction to data visualization came in 1997, when the e-commerce driven Internet bubble was just beginning to pick up momentum. At the time, I was working for an online software retailer in the role of "data analyst." Essentially, this meant that my job was to tell stories using the data being generated from day-to-day operations. My tool of choice was the data visualization technique called an "information dashboard," although at that time I didn't know what I was doing. A dashboard is a visual display of the most important information needed to achieve one or more objectives. In this case it was used by managers to try and understand the forces behind this new thing called "electronic commerce." A dashboard should fit entirely on a single computer screen, or single piece of paper, so that it can be monitored at a glance (Few 2006). At one point I was asked to step into a strategic planning meeting because there was a question about the data I was reporting. Before knocking on the door of the meeting room, I was surprised to overhear an excited conversation taking place inside at top volume. Walking into the meeting it was clear that managers were having an intense conversation with regard to what was happening with the company's sales. Some were very pleased and others were not. The ones who were displeased apparently did not trust the charts and graphs, possibly because it was apparent I had spent too much time trying to make them beautiful and engaging. I was asked several questions and was met with many "ohs" and "ahs" after I explained just what it was they were looking at. I realized three things from that experience. First, the charts and graphs I had assumed were perfectly transparent were anything but. Second, researchers deeply appreciate reporting that drives their curiosity and causes them to think outside of the box and to ask additional questions. Finally, if you have a lot of data and can find a way to make it accessible visually, you can make a researcher very happy. Since that experience I've been interested in understanding both the mechanics and the principles behind information visualization. This chapter discusses what goes into a data visualization and the responsibilities a visualization designer has to the researcher, and demonstrates the process of creating a visualization using Microsoft Excel. This chapter will also spend some time on the principles behind visualizations in an effort to assist librarians in deciding when a data visualization is called for and perhaps necessary (see figure 7.1).

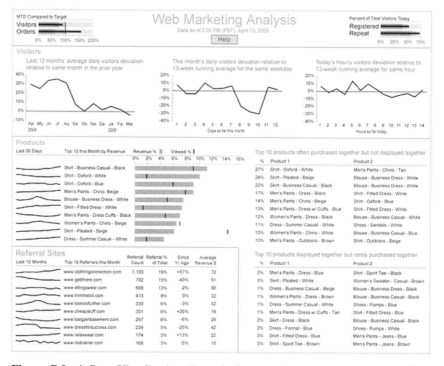

Figure 7.1. A Data Visualization Example from an Information Dashboard (Few 2006).

S. Few, *Information Dashboard Design: the Effective Visual Communication of Data*. Edited by Colleen Wheeler. Sebastopol, CA: O'Reilly Media, Inc., 2006.

INFORMATION AESTHETICS

To begin, it is helpful to position visualizations that are driven by data against other visual communications such as fine art or an illustration. The term *visualization* itself is described as the *act or process of rendering visible* by the *Oxford English Dictionary*. In fine art, what is being rendered is largely mysterious and contextual, but in a data visualization it is entirely discoverable. The reason this distinction is important is because libraries and their stacks of content are often associated with the mysterious as well. Mention "Boolean operators" to any number of people, and you might as well be speaking a foreign language. Data visualization is a powerful communication technique available to anyone with data and a need to use it to tell a story.

The human mind possesses a powerful ability to observe, understand, and respond to images, light, symbols, shapes, patterns, colors, contrast, composition, and balance (Williams 2007). It's possible that this ability has evolved as a necessary response to visual cues within the immediate environment. For example, in a wilderness setting if a person were to encounter a bear, it is quite important to be able to judge not only the animal's position and velocity but also cues such as aggression or indifference. It is equally important that our judgments be the right ones. Data visualization allows us to see certain visual cues plainly and with an understanding that allows us to investigate further to determine next steps. On the other hand, in art the cues are contextual and meanings are always shifting. One might say the power of art stems directly from this uncertainty. But this raises an uncomfortable question since many data visualizations can be said to be beautiful in much the same way as art can be beautiful. Does this mean that a beautiful visualization cannot be trusted in the same way as a spreadsheet full of numbers can be? How can we understand the difference between these two extremes in a way that allows us to build tools that afford certainty?

In a recent paper titled "Towards a Model of Information Aesthetics in Information Visualization" (Lau 2007), the authors make an attempt at modeling the different modes in which visual information is presented. The chart below (figure 7.2) is itself a visualization of visualizations, highlighting the differences in images that live along a continuum between the extremes of concrete and evocative meanings. Let's take a moment to understand the distances between the ideas of "information visualization" and "visualization art."

The vertical axis of the chart, measuring the amount of data focus, shows the ability of an image to communicate concrete information. In the top half of the chart the focus is "extrinsic," meaning that the information is contextual and can only be judged through interpretation and reflection. An example of extrinsic data might be the information conveyed by paint splatters in a Jackson Pollock painting. On the one hand, those splatters are random, but on the other hand they are filled with meaning when taken within the larger context of art history. The information can be found, but it is outside of the

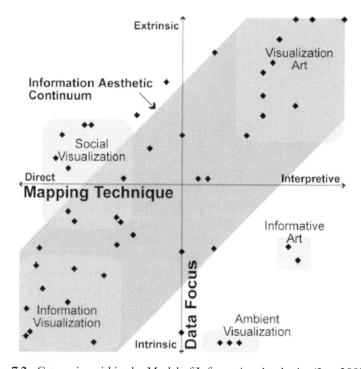

Figure 7.2. Categories within the Model of Information Aesthetics (Lau 2007).

A. Lau and A. Vande Moere, "Towards a Model of Information Aesthetic Visualization," IEEE International Conference on Information Visualisation (IV'07), IEEE, Zurich, Switzerland, 2007, 87–92.

individual paint splatters. In the bottom half of the chart the focus is "intrinsic," meaning the information is embedded in what the visual looks like. An example of intrinsic data would be the measured length of a column of mercury in a glass thermometer. That measurement of length conveys directly the actual temperature. In this example it either is 32 degrees Fahrenheit or it is not. No amount of context or reflection will change this meaning.

Along the horizontal axis, Mapping Technique measures how data is translated to a visual representation. To the right of the vertical axis the translation is interpretive and the supporting data is unavailable to the viewer. An example of interpretive data might be the dance a choreographer designs to convey the emotional tensions of a wedding scene in the movie *The Fiddler on the Roof.* If you'll recall, the father allows his daughters to marry for love instead of insisting on a more traditional arranged marriage. It's an uncertain state of affairs, and in one scene the visual consists of men celebrating the wedding by dancing with bottles balanced atop their heads. The point is that it is impossible for the viewer to discover the father's anxiety by counting the number of bottles balanced on top of the dancers. It's not that the meaning isn't available to the viewer; it is just that the meaning is accessed through interpretation of the context of the scene. And in this case, that would be the delicate act of balancing while dancing. On the other extreme, to the left of the vertical axis the translation of meaning is more direct and the underlying data is accessible. An example might be the visual recommendation system of a book on Amazon.com in which readers have rated the title with an average score of four-and-a-half stars. In this example the meaning can be determined by counting the number of stars given to a book. Furthermore, this average number of stars can be taken apart mathematically to gain further information. Not only can it be shown how many reviews there are, a viewer can also drill down both to see the types of people who have rated the book and to read the reviews for themselves. In this example the meaning of the visualization is direct and accessible.

According to this model, information visualization occurs in the lower left quadrant of the chart. In that area the visual content of an image equals the meaning of the data. Furthermore, the elements of a visual can be reliably taken apart to reveal additional information. It is this affordance to discover, to "take apart," the underlying data that is the hallmark of data visualization. And with this model we have shown that while an image may be beautiful, it doesn't necessarily follow that the image cannot reliably carry concrete information.

DYNAMIC INTERACTION

It may be that multiple views of the data which are highly interactive, extensively interlinked, and immediately responsive—and which are intimately linked with the actions of the user—provide the best chance for accurate insight. This highly dynamic interactivity can change the data analyst's view of the data by providing new information effortlessly. (Young 2006)

The ability to take apart a visualization has some consequences on the design of the visual image. The designers of data visualizations need to have a certain amount of integrity with regard to the work they are doing. This is because the user of a data visualization will depend on both the accuracy of the underlying data as well as the visual representation, which conveys meaning. First we'll take a look at what is expected of a visualization, and then we'll define the data elements required to meet those expectations. Finally, in the following section, we'll walk through the process of designing a visualization that will pull everything together.

The paradigm for interactivity in any given visualization boils down to allowing for these three "activities of seeing" (Young 2006):

1. *Visual Exploration:* Librarians are familiar with the power of serendipity. By allowing users the ability to explore data, serendipitous discoveries will end up inspiring the user to generate hypotheses "on the fly" and then to immediately test these against the available data.

2. *Visual Transformation:* Hidden patterns can be discovered by allowing the user to adjust data elements. An example of this action might involve a visualization

of library items that have been checked out during the spring semester and then presented organized by subject terms. The user may want to follow a hunch and transform the date element to show only items checked out during the week immediately before spring break and then include all data from previous years to look for trends.

3. *Visual Impact:* Many designers make the mistake of trying to "dress up" a report with clip art or other elements that have no relationship to the underlying data. The reason for this may be because of a lack of confidence in the underlying data. A well-designed visualization allows the data itself to provide the drama. The goal is to allow the user an "aha!" moment as the result of seeing data in a new and surprising way.

To allow for the exploration, transformation, and impact of visualizations, data needs to be available to the user in the following three modes (Ware 2000):

1. *Entities:* These are the objects of interest to the user. Examples might include the book holdings of a library, Twitter or Facebook profiles, or the stock prices of publicly traded companies, and so forth.

2. *Relationships:* These are the structures that relate entities to each other. Relationships can be either causal or temporal. A causal relationship measures how entities affect one another. As an example, the number of books checked out by freshman as opposed to seniors would be measured by the relationship between student seniority entities as well as "check out" entities.

3. *Attributes:* These are essentially the metadata of both entities and relationships. "Nominal" attributes identify labeling such as "freshman." "Ordinal" attributes quantify with values, such as the number of books checked out. "Interval" is an attribute that is useful for identifying gaps in data, such as "semester," "month," or even check out periods. "Ratio" is a comparison to zero, such as the ratio of freshmen with overdue fines.

The chart below (figure 7.3) illustrates the three modes of data that make up a visualization. This is a tag cloud that visualizes the frequency of a given

Figure 7.3. A Visualization of Weblog Postings (McCann, 2009).

keyword in relation to other keywords. The more often a keyword is present, the larger the font. Hovering over a keyword allows the viewer to see the individual event titles that make up the tag. The entities here are the events themselves, represented by keywords found in the title of the events. The relationships are between library entities who are scheduling similar events. The attributes being measured are nominal keywords and the ordinal counts of occurrences, represented by the size of the fonts.

PRINCIPLES OF DESIGN

In his seminal book *The Visual Display of Quantitative Information* (2001), Edward R. Tufte describes the five principles of good graphics. Let's review these and then walk through the creation of a visualization using his principles.

1. *Above all else show the data:* In the word cloud above, figure 7.3, the data is represented vividly by the size of the fonts. The greater the number of events being represented by a certain keyword, the larger the font is for that keyword.

2. *Maximize the data to "ink" ratio:* Tufte describes this as the proportion of the total ink, or pixels as the case may be, used to create a graphic to the total ink used to represent actual data. His point is that ink present in a visualization that is not related to actual data is both a waste and detriment to the users' understanding of the information. Again, figure 7.3 is an excellent example of a high ratio of data-ink to overall ink.

3. *Erase nondata ink:* This principle is fairly straightforward; if your data-ink ratio is not high enough simply get rid of nondata ink.

4. *Erase redundant data-ink:* It is possible that in some instances, redundant data is necessary, but this mostly relates to schedules. For example, some libraries are open from early in the morning to early the following morning. A visualization of open hours might be confusing if instead of "Wednesday, 7 am–2 am" it instead showed "Wednesday, 7 am–Thursday, 2 am." It's reasonable to assume that students wanting to study from midnight to 2 am on a Wednesday night would not search a visual schedule under "Thursday."

5. *Revise and Edit:* This is more difficult than it at first sounds. Knowing what data-ink is fat, and what is lean, requires multiple iterations of editing.

In order to further illustrate some of the decisions that need to be made with any data visualization, let's walk through the creation of an example in figure 7.4.

Using the above example data set, we'll pretend that we're building a tool that allows administrators to visualize the amount of inbound interlibrary loans for a given year, with a couple of subject headings as relationships. Using an extreme example, the resulting tool may end up looking something like figure 7.5.

This is an example of good intentions run amok. The first thing that jumps out at the viewer is what is known as "chart junk" defined as optical art,

Year	Accounting, General	Computer games, video games	Grand Total
2003	28	0	33
2004	7	2	13
2005	12	6	28
2006	2	3	13
2007	3	6	18
2008	2	3	12
Grand Total	54	20	117

Figure 7.4. Hypothetical Data Set Showing Interlibrary Loan Figures for Two Subjects versus the Total of All Loans.

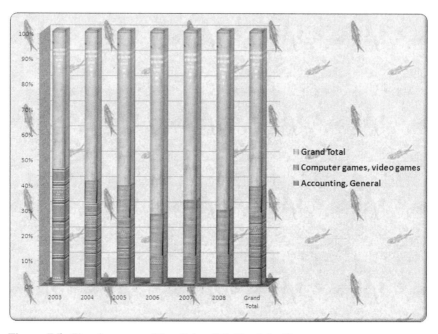

Figure 7.5. First Attempt at Visualizing ILL Totals by Year.

whether intentional or not, that has little-to-no data value (Tufte 2001). In this example, there are clip art fossilized fish as background and book spine graphics representing percentage totals. Additionally, the chart visualization is set up using a false third dimension along the Z axis. There is no data-derived reason to have this axis because it isn't present in the underlying data. The user of the tool cannot drill down along the Z axis to retrieve more data. All in all, the effect of the visualization is one of visual interference, a vibration set up by the conflict between elements that have meaning and those elements that do not.

To rescue this visualization, the next step is to maximize the data-to-ink ratio. We'll do this by first erasing all nondata ink (see figure 7.6).

In the above example we've removed the "chart junk": the clip art fish, the book spines, and the false third dimension. What we have left is a great improvement over the original. The next step, according to Tufte, is to revise and edit. Taking another hard look at the image, it becomes apparent that there is still ink that is unrelated to actual data. For example, the Y axis contains multiple hash marks denoting increments of apparently two percent. In addition, both the Y and X axes have lines which act as borders to the chart where the data lives. In the process of taking a hard look, our next revision removes these visual elements which we've determined are not associated with data (see figure 7.7).

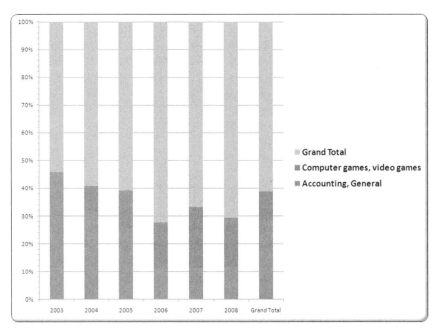

Figure 7.6. Second Attempt at Visualizing ILL Totals by Year.

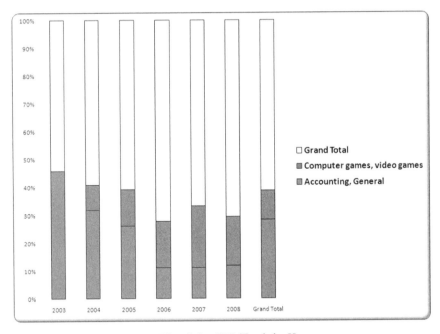

Figure 7.7. Final Attempt at Visualizing ILL Totals by Year.

As you can see, removing the last of the nondata ink had a profound effect on the chart. The borders along the Y and X axes were doing very little to help with understanding the data. By removing the horizontal lines in the center of the chart, we've removed a visual grid "vibration" effect that was interfering with interpretation of the data. Even without the horizontal guides the eye can still compare the Y axis to any of the columns to make a reasonable judgment with regard to the value of the column.

In this example what we've accomplished, when we look back at the Information Aesthetic model of figure 7.2, is to move the visualization from the upper-right quadrant down to the lower left. By removing chart junk, we've removed elements in the visualization that cannot be interpreted directly. By filtering out the false three dimensions and clip art images that have no data associated with them, we've made the image more reliable and concrete. In this sense, we have lived up to what Young terms the "Four Respects" (Young 2006):

1. *Respect people*—All visual data, or "data ink," according to Tufte, must be able to be understood accurately and intuitively. The fossilized fish in the background of figure 7.5 was an interesting touch, but it created serious barriers to understanding meaning. It was an element that could not be directly understood, only interpreted as background noise.

2. *Respect Data*—Each data type must have an appropriate visualization. In our example we used a vertical bar to represent the ratio of zero to 100 percent. We could also have used pie charts, one for each year, and that would also have been an appropriate visualization.

3. *Respect Mathematics*—The algebra of mathematical statistics must be translated into the geometry of statistical visualization. In our original example, the chart was built with a third dimensional element that violated this principle.

4. *Respect Computers*—The analyst's interaction with the data must be immediate and smooth, thereby affording creative interpretation by the analyst. Because this was a static example, we were not in any danger of violating this "respect." However, if this were to be set up as a tool that queried interlibrary loan data on the fly, we might run into a problem. In order for any visualization to be effective, it needs to afford both visual exploration and transformation. If the computer needs to make a call back to a couple databases and then reanalyze the data from scratch each and every time, the chances are that it would not be a smooth process unless steps were taken to optimize the data transformations on the back end. Any frustration felt by the user of a visualization would violate this "respect."

VISUALIZATION: PROBLEMS AND POTENTIAL

By now we have an understanding of where data visualizations fall within the spectrum of visual communication. We also have an idea of what it takes to create an effective visualization. It's possible that you may already have an idea, or several, about how library data can be used in a visualization. However, I'm not convinced that data visualizations are an exact science. This is evidenced by a panel discussion conducted at the conference *IEEE Visualization 2004*, where leading researchers in the field of visualization were asked to come up with the top 10 unsolved information visualization problems (Chen 2005). I've included them below, with limited discussion, because they are problems librarians and other information professionals will need to address as well.

1. *Usability*—Thinking in terms of what the designer of a product has in mind compared to what the user actually experiences will always be a central problem. All visualization tools developed within the library world will need to factor in a user-centered approach as a cost of doing business.

2. *Understanding elementary perceptual-cognitive tasks*—In building our example visualization, several nondata ink elements were removed without a real understanding of the extent of harm they were doing. For example, what is our confidence level with regard to removing the horizontal grid as Tufte suggested? This is an area ripe for further study.

3. *Prior knowledge*—Libraries are faced with some interesting challenges as a profession. We are blessed with an enormous amount of data in terms of information buried deep within the stacks. In any given subject, how do we build

visualization tools that allow our users to drill down deeply within a given knowledge domain, and without bewildering our users?

4. *Education and training*—We do have a history in this area; specifically I'm thinking of the visualization training that went into the hand-typed catalog cards. Each of those cards represents a series of design decisions and an awareness of both the potential and problems inherent in a catalog record. More thought is needed in this area to increase the user's at-a-glance perception of a library's holdings. We do have static OPAC records but are lacking in terms of allowing on-the-fly visualizations and transformations of the library's data.

5. *Intrinsic quality measures*—Currently, there are no quality metrics that I'm aware of for visualizations other than the ones discussed here.

6. *Scalability*—Not only are libraries sitting on vast quantities of information, we also have available equally vast quantities of supporting data and metadata to incorporate. One example is the availability of social network data. It is possible to envision a tool being built that integrates the impact factors of not only journal articles but also of books, weblogs, and other forms of communications outside of the scholarly publishing paradigm. With that much data, scalability will be a challenge.

7. *Aesthetics*—Libraries are custodians to all sorts of quantitative data, but we are also responsible for work done within the arts. In the example given earlier of the interpretive choreography found in *The Fiddler on the Roof,* it is known that the dance does carry a significant amount of information. It is just hidden to databases. How will metadata be constructed for these types of aesthetics? How will that information then be visualized in a useful way?

8. *Paradigm shift: structures to dynamics*—Journal impact factors are conceivably simple to quantify and visualize. What is more difficult is bringing in temporal trends. For example, the recession that began in 2008 caught many authorities by surprise even though analysts supposedly had access to roughly the same data. How is it possible to visualize authoritative opinion as it evolves over time?

9. *Causality, visual inference, and predictions*—When working with a visualization tool of any kind, the user needs to be able to judge between background noise and meaningful data. How will this be done without a deep understanding of individual subject domains?

10. *Knowledge domain visualization*—Again, it is relatively simple to show impact factors, but what is more of a challenge is targeting the social constructions that identify certain works as crucial within a given field.

CONCLUSION

In this chapter we discussed the elements of a data visualization and the responsibilities a visualization designer has to the researcher, and demonstrated a simple version of the process for creating a visualization. We also spent some time on the background principles behind visualizations and dealt with briefly some of the coming challenges. The important thing to remember is the effect that good visualizations have upon the researcher. Allowing the researcher to experience a genuine "aha" moment as the result of seeing data under new light will be a challenging and highly rewarding endeavor.

REFERENCES

Chen, C. "Top 10 Unsolved Information Visualization Problems." *IEEE Computer Graphics and Applications* 25, no. 4 (2005): 12–16.

Few, S. *Information Dashboard Design: the Effective Visual Communication of Data.* Edited by Colleen Wheeler. Sebastopol, CA: O'Reilly Media, 2006.

Lau, A., and, A. V. Moere. *Towards a Model of Information Aesthetic in Information Visualization.* IEEE International Conference on Information Visualization (IV'07), IEEE, Zurich, Switzerland, 2007, 87–92.

McCann, Steve. *A Digital Outrigger.* Available from http://librarydigitalprojects. com/about/tag-cloud (Accessed 8/25/2009).

Shirky, Clay. "It's Not Information Overload. It's Filter Failure." [video] *Web 2.0 Expo,* New York, 2008. Available from http://www.web2expo.com/webexny2008/ public/schedule/detail/4817.

Tufte, Edward R. *The Visual Display of Quantitative Information,* 2nd ed. Cheshire, CT: Graphics Press, 2001.

Ware, Colin. *Information Visualization: Perception for Design.* San Francisco, CA: Morgan Kaufman, 2000.

Williams, Rick, and Julianne H. Newton. *Visual Communication : Integrating Media, Art and Science.* New York: Lawrence Erlbaum Associates, 2007.

Young, Forrest W., Pedro Valero-Mora, and Michael Friendly. *Visual Statistics: Seeing Data with Dynamic Interactive Graphics.* Hoboken, NJ: Wiley-Interscience, 2006.

ADDITIONAL READING

Arnheim, Rudolf. *Visual Thinking.* Berkeley: University of California Press, 1969.

Bederson, Benjamin, and Ben Shneiderman. *The Craft of Information Visualization: Readings and Reflections.* San Francisco, CA; Oxford, UK: Morgan Kaufmann; Elsevier Science, 2003.

Huff, Darrell. *How to Lie with Statistics.* New York: Norton, 1993.

IBM. *Many Eyes for Shared Visualization and Discovery.* 2009 Available from http:// manyeyes.alphaworks.ibm.com/manyeyes/ (Retrieved 3/30/2009).

Spence, Robert. *Information Visualization.* Harlow, UK: Addison-Wesley, 2001.

Wilkinson, Leland. *The Grammar of Graphics.* New York: Springer, 1999.

Wurman, Richard S. *Information Anxiety.* New York: Doubleday, 1989.

SELECTED VISUALIZATION EXAMPLES

Crazy Egg: http://www.crazyegg.com/
Datavisualization: http://www.datavisualization.ch
Gap Minder: http://www.gapminder.org/
Information Aesthetics: http://infosthetics.com/
Lexipedia: http://www.lexipedia.com/

Many Eyes: http://manyeyes.alphaworks.ibm.com/manyeyes/
A Periodic Table of Visualization Methods: http://www.visual-literacy.org/periodic_
    table/periodic_table.html
Thinkmap Visual Thesaurus: http://www.visualthesaurus.com/
Visual Complexity: http://www.visualcomplexity.com/vc/
Visuwords Online Graphical Dictionary: http://www.visuwords.com/
WallStats: http://www.wallstats.com/
WikiMindMap: http://www.wikimindmap.org/
World Mapper: http://www.worldmapper.org/

8

SORTING THROUGH DIGITAL PRESERVATION SYSTEMS

Ardys Kozbial

Data deluge has become a current buzzword for those working in the areas of digital preservation and data curation, as well as those in computer science, libraries, and archives. The phrase sounds scary and threatening, especially when those who use it seem like alarmists with no helpful solutions for short- or long-term management of data and other digital assets.

According to an International Data Corporation (IDC) white paper, 2007 marked a "crossover" year, when there were more digital data created than data storage to host them. The IDC report also projected that by 2011 the amount of digital data created will be more than twice the amount of available storage (Gantz 2008).

While it is true that data are being created at an astonishing rate, there are groups concentrating on various aspects of the problem, from economic (Blue Ribbon Task Force) to digital preservation (National Digital Information Infrastructure Preservation Program) to data curation (DigCCur, UIUC Data Curation) to the scientific method (Anderson 2008). This chapter will take a closer look at this data deluge and its relationship to libraries and archives. What are these data? Why do libraries and archives care? What do they need to understand? What role do librarians and archivists play in long-term data management?

DIGITAL PRESERVATION

Since the field of digital preservation is relatively young, terminology and meaning continue to be in flux, making it worthwhile to provide some clarification at the beginning.

For the purposes of this chapter, digital data can range from cultural heritage data to raw scientific data sets to e-journals to geospatial data. Cultural heritage data is generally associated with the humanities and often refers to data found in digital libraries, for example, digitized versions of images, books, archival material, and artworks, as well as born digital versions of the same.

The following three definitions of digital preservation will serve as the basis for the discussion in the rest of this chapter.

> Digital preservation combines policies, strategies and actions that ensure access to information in digital formats over time. (American Library Association)
>
> [Digital preservation r]efers to the series of managed activities necessary to ensure continued access to digital materials for as long as necessary. (Digital Preservation Coalition)
>
> Digital preservation is the series of actions and interventions required to ensure continued and reliable access to authentic digital objects for as long as they are deemed to be of value. (Joint Information Systems Committee 2006)

What makes a data backup different from digital preservation? Backups are typically stored in a single location (often on a server near that which is being backed up) and are performed only periodically. Backups are designed to address short-term data loss via minimal investment of money and staff resources. Backups are better than nothing but not a comprehensive solution to the problem of preserving information over time. Digital preservation is strategic. Preserving information over long periods of time requires systematic attention rather than benign neglect or unthinking actions (Halbert 2008).

CHALLENGES TO SUSTAINABLE DIGITAL PRESERVATION AND ACCESS

The Blue Ribbon Task Force on Sustainable Digital Preservation and Access was commissioned in 2008 to identify sustainable economic models to provide access to the ever-growing amount of digital information in the public interest. Its interim report lists systemic challenges that create barriers for sustainable digital access and preservation. They are paraphrased here and can be found in their complete form in the report (Blue Ribbon Task Force 2008).

Inadequacy of funding models to address long-term access and preservation needs. There is a need for persistent digital access and preservation funding.

Confusion and/or lack of alignment between stakeholders' roles and responsibilities with respect to digital access and preservation. It is often the case that those who create and use digital information are distinct from those who serve as its stewards and support its preservation and access.

Inadequate institutional, enterprise, and/or community incentives to support the collaboration needed to reinforce sustainable economic models. Digital preservation and access require long-range planning and support, agreement on formats, standards and use models, interoperability of relevant hardware and software systems, and partnering among a diverse group of technologists, users, data center staff, compliance officers, financial managers, and the like.

Complacency that current practices are good enough. The urgency of developing sustainable economic models for digital information is not uniformly appreciated.

Fear that digital access and preservation is too big to take on. There is general agreement that in its entirety digital preservation is a big problem, incorporating technical, economic, regulatory, policy, social, and other aspects. But it is not insurmountable. Digital access and preservation may be as manageable as including a "data bill" as an explicit and fixed part of an institution's business model.

WHY SHOULD LIBRARIANS AND ARCHIVISTS CARE ABOUT DIGITAL PRESERVATION?

Given this overwhelming problem of a data deluge, the definitions of digital preservation, and the challenges to digital preservation and access, why should librarians and archivists engage with them? Why should they care? Why not let these issues fall into the realm of computer scientists and other technologists?

Librarians and archivists must protect their investments. Consider digital libraries. Libraries and archives have made a considerable investment in digitizing their collections in order to make them accessible on the Web, and most have a collection of digital assets. If these digital assets are not managed for the long term, how much will it cost to redigitize those materials, provided that they could be digitized again.

Whether reports, digital images, or dissertations, every library has a collection of "born digital" materials among its digital assets. These materials do not necessarily have an analog (nondigital) equivalent. They are part of the library or archives' holdings and must be managed for the long term in the same way that analog materials are managed for the long term.

Academic administrations are looking to their libraries and archives to manage raw data (mostly scientific at this juncture). In essence they are saying to academic libraries, "You are librarians and archivists. You are the keepers of the scholarly record. Here's the new scholarly record." Fifty years ago, Professor X's notebooks of oceanographic data collected on board a ship might have found their way to the archives to be interpreted and reused by researchers in the future. Today, that professor's data are transmitted from the ship to servers on campus (for example, the Scripps Institution of Oceanography). Reuse will be possible only if the data are preserved for the long term.

WHAT ROLE(S) CAN LIBRARIANS AND ARCHIVISTS PLAY?

An important opportunity that the problem of digital preservation has exposed is that of collaboration. Computer scientists and technologists cannot address the problem alone, nor can librarians and archivists, nor can researchers and faculty. All of these groups are learning to work together with the common goal of ensuring that data are managed for the long term.

Looking at the definitions of digital preservation above, where do librarians and archivists fit in? In other words, what are they good at? Librarians and archivists are great at making and carrying out policy. In their public service role, they excel at reliable access to information. In their appraisal activities, they constantly make judgment calls about what is "deemed to be of value" and how long is "as long as necessary."

In the Blue Ribbon Task Force list of challenges, it is the areas that require long-range planning that bring librarians and archivists into the mix of collaborators. Librarians and archivists are taught to consider the accessibility of information in hundred-year periods; technologists are not. Related to this long-term view is the Blue Ribbon challenge that "it is often the case that those who create and use digital information are distinct from those who serve as its stewards and support its preservation and access." Librarians and archivists are almost always in this position and surely can offer strategies for meeting this challenge.

WHAT DO LIBRARIANS AND ARCHIVISTS NEED TO KNOW ABOUT DIGITAL PRESERVATION?

In order to participate actively in digital preservation, librarians and archivists need to become familiar with national and international organizations working in this area as well as keep up with the variety of active digital preservation systems and repositories.

Two words, *access* and *users*, seem to cause confusion and must be defined when considering systems and repositories. Librarians and archivists are accustomed to thinking of the general public as its user, but the general public is almost never the user of a digital preservation system. Librarians and archivists would like their institution's digital assets to be available 24/7, but digital preservation systems are not set up for this kind of accessibility, and expectations must often be managed. With this in mind, the audience must be carefully agreed upon.

When assessing digital preservation systems, librarians and archivists should consider the following:

- Does the institution have adequate technical support to build its own system?
- If the institution wants to outsource digital preservation, how does it know it can trust the digital repository it chooses?

DIGITAL PRESERVATION SYSTEMS

In a well-informed special issue of *Library Technology Reports* devoted to the preservation of digital materials, Priscilla Caplan begins to sort out some of the available digital preservation options. "Most available systems, including

DSpace, EPrints, and Fedora, are institutional repository (IR) applications designed to collect and disseminate the intellectual output of a university or other academic institution. DAITSS and LOCKSS differ from the IR applications in that preservation is their primary function. DAITSS is a 'dark archive,' a preservation repository with no end-user interface, built strictly along the OAIS model. LOCKSS is an automated mechanism for harvesting and ensuring the integrity of Web-accessible content, primarily e-journals. aDORe is a solution to the storage component of a preservation repository"(Caplan 2008).

One very important component of a digital preservation system is the replication aspect. Computer scientists agree that the best method of preserving digital data is by managing multiple copies of them. Debated issues include: How many copies are the right amount? Should the copies be geographically dispersed? Which are the best places to disperse them, and which technology or technologies are the most reliable?

New projects, products, and their acronyms come through in-boxes at a rapid pace, and the next several sections attempt to sort through some of them. This is not a comprehensive list. When announcements are posted or presentations are made at conferences, potential users should first ask themselves, what is it? Is this a piece of software that an institution's information technology department can run? Is this a repository where an institution can send its digital assets? If it is a repository, to which institutions is it applicable? For example, Portico focuses on "scholarly literature published in electronic form, beginning with scholarly journals" (Portico 2009). Or, is this new acronym a research group, a national or international digital preservation association, or a commercial venture?

Other than Chronopolis, the descriptions of the following applications, repositories, and assessment efforts are necessarily brief. They undergo constant change, and it is best to refer to the individual Web sites for the most current information.

SOFTWARE APPLICATIONS

Dark Archive in the Sunshine State (DAITSS)

The DAITSS overview describes the system as follows:

DAITSS is a digital preservation repository application developed by the Florida Center for Library Automation. In addition to repository functions of ingest, data management and dissemination, DAITSS supports the preservation functions of format normalization, mass format migration, and migration on request.

DAITSS is a "dark archive" intended to be used as a back-end to other systems, such as digital library applications or institutional repository software. It has no public interface and allows no public access, but it can be used in conjunction with an access system. (DAITSS 2007)

DAITSS version 1.5 is in production, meaning that it can be downloaded and used. Version 2.0 is currently under development. DAITSS is available as open source software under the GPL license.[1] This is a piece of software that an institution's information technology department may run. It is the underlying software for the Florida Digital Archive, which is described below in the Repository section.

LOCKSS

Lots of Copies Keep Stuff Safe (LOCKSS), based at Stanford University, is the name of a software technology as well as the community that uses it. According to the LOCKSS Web site, this is what the software does.

A library uses LOCKSS software to turn a low-cost PC into a digital preservation appliance called a LOCKSS Box that performs the following four functions:

> It collects content from the target web sites using a web crawler similar to those used by search engines.
>
> It continually compares the content it has collected with the same content collected by other LOCKSS Boxes, and repairs any differences.
>
> It acts as a web proxy or cache, providing browsers in the library's community with access to the publisher's content or the preserved content as appropriate. It can also serve content by Metadata (Open URLs) via resolvers.
>
> It provides a web-based administrative interface that allows the library staff to target new journals for preservation, monitor the state of the journals being preserved, and control access to the preserved journals. (LOCKSS How It Works 2009)

When a library adds a LOCKSS Box to its information technology department, it becomes part of a LOCKSS network, which is discussed in the Repository section.

Storage Resource Broker

The Storage Resource Broker (SRB) is "a client-server middleware that provides a uniform interface for connecting to heterogeneous data resources over a network and accessing unique or replicated data objects" (Schroeder 2004).

This is a complex and powerful piece of software developed by the Data Intensive Cyber Environments group (DICE 2009). Two aspects of SRB that make it particularly useful to libraries are its scalability and its focus on long-term preservation. For the scalability aspect, SRB can manage millions of files and terabytes of data. For the long-term preservation aspect, the designers of the system created it with the understanding that long- term preservation from the librarian and archivist point of view is in perpetuity.

Integrated Rule-Oriented Data System

The Integrated Rule-Oriented Data System (iRODS) "management policies (sets of assertions these communities make about their digital collections) are characterized in iRODS Rules and state information. At the iRODS core, a Rule Engine interprets the Rules to decide how the system is to respond to various requests and conditions. iRODS is open source under a BSD license"[2] (iRODS 2009).

In a very simple archival example, iRODS works as follows. According to the policies of the Billing Department of University X, it saves certain transactions for five years and then destroys them. (All transactions are electronic and there are no paper records.) A rule is created in iRODS that forces those records to be reviewed in five years. The fact that they may be destroyed is brought to the archivist's attention, and the archivist may delete the files. Multiply this one policy by all the records policies for electronic records and you'll get an idea of how iRODS works. Like SRB, it is complex, but once the rules are set up and automated, it is a powerful tool.

aDORe

The digital preservation system aDORe is a federated framework that includes a storage methodology aiming to address scalability issues in large-scale digital repositories. It is a group of software applications that can be used to build a repository (aDORe 2009).

REPOSITORIES

Florida Digital Archive

According to the Florida Digital Archive's (FDA) Policy Guide, its mission is as follows:

> The mission of the Florida Digital Archive (FDA) is to provide a cost effective, long-term preservation repository for digital materials in support of teaching and learning, scholarship, and research in the state of Florida.
>
> In support of this mission, the FDA guarantees that all files deposited by agreement with its affiliates remain available, unaltered, and readable from media. For those materials designated to receive full preservation treatment, the FDA will maintain a usable version using the best format migration tools available. (Florida Digital Archive, 2007)

Institutions interested in depositing their digital material with the FDA may consult its policy guide and contact the FDA directly.

LOCKSS

LOCKSS is a community approach to digital preservation and describes the approach this way:

> LOCKSS helps libraries stay relevant by building collections even as an increasing portion of today's content is born digitally and published on the web.
>
> LOCKSS replicates the traditional model of libraries keeping physical copies of books, journals, etc. in their collections, making it possible for libraries to house copies of digital materials long term. (LOCKSS Home 2009)

Each institution with a LOCKSS Box is cooperating and sharing data with other institutions that gather content on a LOCKSS Box.

MetaArchive

The MetaArchive Cooperative is building Trusted Digital Repositories using LOCKSS software to provide long-term care for digital materials. MetaArchive functions as a community initiative, meaning that there is information technology participation among the members and each institution commits to managing a LOCKSS Box.

According to its Web site, MetaArchive's

> collaborative networks are comprised of libraries, archives, and other cultural heritage institutions that seek to cooperatively preserve their digital materials, not by outsourcing to other organizations, but by actively participating in the preservation of their own content.
>
> How we do it. To preserve digital assets, the MetaArchive Cooperative uses a systemic, forward-looking technological approach called distributed digital preservation. Our member institutions identify collections that they want to preserve. Using a technical framework that is based on the LOCKSS (Lots of Copies Keep Stuff Safe) software, these collections are then ingested into a geographically distributed network where they are stored on secure file servers in multiple locations. These servers do not merely back up the materials, but rather provide a dynamic means of constantly checking each file and providing repairs whenever necessary. (MetaArchive, About 2009)

Portico

Portico's mission is very specifically to "preserve scholarly literature published in electronic form and to ensure that these materials remain accessible to future scholars, researchers, and students" (Portico, About 2007).

Libraries and archives do not deposit their own materials with Portico but are asked to pay an annual fee to help sustain Portico's service.

> The Portico service offers a permanent archive of electronic scholarly journals, e-books, d[igitized]-newspapers, and local library content, thereby providing protection against the potential loss of access to e-literature integral to a library's collection.
>
> Portico provides all libraries supporting the archive with campus-wide access to archived content when specific trigger events occur, and when titles are no longer available from the publisher or other source. Trigger events include:
>
> A publisher stops operations; or
>
> A publisher ceases to publish a title, or
>
> A publisher no longer offers back issues, or
>
> Upon catastrophic and sustained failure of a publisher's delivery platform.

Portico also provides a reliable means to secure perpetual access, if participating publishers choose to designate Portico as a provider of post-cancellation
access. In addition, select librarians at participating libraries are granted
password-controlled access for verification and audit purposes only. (Portico,
Service 2009)

In this approach to digital preservation, libraries and archives leave all of the
technical work to the repository.

Chronopolis

Since this author is most familiar with the Chronopolis preservation environment, it will be described in more detail here. All of the repositories and applications mentioned in this chapter have the same goal: keeping data and digital
assets safe for the long term. The policies and parameters established by each
of these repositories and applications differentiate them. There is no single
agreed-upon approach in either the library and archives community or among
computer scientists, and all systems mentioned here are working fine thus far.

Chronopolis (2009) is a digital preservation environment as well as the
name of a project funded by the National Digital Information Infrastructure
Preservation Program (NDIIPP 2009) at the Library of Congress. The project is building this preservation environment within a grid-based network that
holds data from institutions other than the partner institutions. The partners
store and manage the data in the system as a service to the data providers.

The partner institutions in Chronopolis are the University of California
San Diego (the San Diego Supercomputer Center (SDSC) and the UCSD
Libraries), the University of Maryland Institute for Advanced Computer
Studies (UMIACS), and the National Center for Atmospheric Research
(NCAR). The partner institutions are responsible for storage and network
support, maintaining a copy of all the data at each institution, network testing,
metadata expertise, and support for the SRB, the Replication Monitor (Repli-
cation Monitor 2009), and the Audit Control Environment (ACE 2009).

Like LOCKSS (the repository) and MetaArchive, Chronopolis replicates its
data in geographically dispersed areas. For LOCKSS and MetaArchive, geographic distribution is as disparate as the collaborating members (LOCKSS,
Service 2009; MetaArchive, Current 2009). For Chronopolis, the partners
are located in San Diego, California; College Park, Maryland; and Boulder,
Colorado. While none of the other repositories declare a set number of replicated copies, Chronopolis policy states a total of three replicas.

The underlying software for MetaArchive and LOCKSS is LOCKSS; the
underlying software for the FDA is DAITSS; and the underlying software for
Chronopolis is SRB. Chronopolis plans to migrate to iRODS but not in the current phase of the project. While the Chronopolis partners use the same underlying software, as another failure-prevention measure the hardware is varied.
SDSC and NCAR use Sun machines, and UMIACS uses Apple hardware.

Finally, all of the systems use automated monitoring systems. For Chronopolis, the Replication Monitor is constantly checking to make sure that all three copies of the data are the same. By definition, the copy of the data that resides at SDSC is the master copy and the other two must match it. This is a policy decision and not a technical one. Any one of the copies could be the master. ACE is a second monitoring system that checks each replica. There is an ACE monitor running at each site. In the summer of 2009, a Web site will be launched that will allow the data providers to check the monitors to see that systems are working well.

The data providers for Chronopolis include the California Digital Library (CDL), the Inter-university Consortium for Political and Social Research (ICPSR) at the University of Michigan, North Carolina State University (NCSU), and the Scripps Institution of Oceanography (SIO) at UCSD. All of the data providers are also NDIIPP Partners, and all of the data ingested into Chronopolis are related to NDIIPP projects.

CDL (CDL 2009), a department of the University of California's Office of the President (UCOP), provides centralized support for digital initiatives that serve all of the libraries in the University of California system. CDL contributed five terabytes of data to Chronopolis from its Web-at-Risk project, which has been comprised of web crawls of political and governmental Web sites over the course of five years. The web crawler packages the data into files of uniform size.

Chronopolis is managing ICPSR's (ICPSR 2009) complete holdings, consisting of approximately eight terabytes of data. This collection includes 40 years of social science research data comprised of millions of small files.

NCSU's (2009) data include approximately six terabytes of state and local geospatial data that were collected under the auspices of the North Carolina Geospatial Data Archiving Project, one of the initial eight NDIIPP projects. NCSU is also part of NDIIPP's new multistate effort, which is keenly interested in exchange of digital content among states.

SIO's (2009) one terabyte of data consists of data gathered from approximately 1,000 SIO research expeditions during the past 50 years. SIO was able to combine these data into one place with the help of a Digital Archiving (DigArch) research grant from NDIIPP.

By the end of spring 2009, Chronopolis will be nearly filled to its 50-terabyte capacity allotted in the first phase. These data present themselves in a wide variety of file formats, and the content includes web crawls, geospatial data, social science data, atmospheric/oceanographic data, and cultural-heritage data. The Chronopolis partners purposely solicited a diverse set of data content and types in order to develop and test Chronopolis's capacity to manage efficiently and reliably.

All of the repositories mentioned here have varying policies that limit or define the data that are included in the repository. The FDA seems to be concentrating on data that have a connection to the state of Florida, but it doesn't seem to be particular about the format or content. LOCKSS is focused on gathering and preserving web-based data but doesn't have a geographic limit. MetaArchive is interested in data from cultural-heritage institutions and, because it uses LOCKSS, the data will be web-based. However, the MetaArchive members are internationally dispersed. LOCKSS and MetaArchive also require heavy technical participation by member institutions. Portico is concerned with preservation of scholarly literature and requires monetary participation by members in order to sustain the service, but little technical participation.

Chronopolis would like to expand its roster of data providers (it currently serves only NDIIPP partners) but will take any format or size of data set.

While librarians and archivists do not need to have a deep technical understanding of these systems, they must understand system policies. Most importantly, they must have an understanding of their own data in order to match their data to the preservation system that will work best for their situation.

TRUSTING THE SYSTEMS

There are two major efforts underway to standardize digital repository auditing. In the United States, the Trustworthy Repositories Audit and Certification: Criteria and Checklist is centered at the Center for Research Libraries (CRL) (TRAC 2009). Currently, there is no independent auditing and certification body. Preservation repositories may complete the checklist internally to find their strengths and weaknesses. CRL has also made an effort to audit a few repositories and to issue reports (CRL 2009). Librarians and archivists should become familiar with these reports in order to make good decisions about their own preservation repositories. If an institution is considering building its own preservation repository, can it comply with the checklist? If not, perhaps an external or third-party repository should be considered.

The second is a European Union effort called Digital Repository Audit Method Based on Risk Assessment (DRAMBORA 2009). This group has recently released an interactive tool kit that facilitates internal audit of a preservation system. Again, there is no independent certification and auditing body, but both of these efforts provide a start for preservation repositories to assess themselves.

CONCLUSION

Librarians and archivists need to pay attention to the data deluge. They will be asked to participate actively in collaborative efforts to preserve these data because they are well qualified in some of the preservation activities. While librarians and archivists don't have to build their own digital preservation systems, they do need to have the tools and information to make a good assessment of existing systems.

NOTES

1. GNU General Public License. For more information see http://www.gnu.org/copyleft/gpl.html (retrieved April 6, 2009).

2. A permissive family of software licenses with fewer restrictions that the GPL license. For more information see http://en.wikipedia.org/wiki/BSD_license (retrieved April 6, 2009).

REFERENCES

aDORe. *aDORe Projects,* 2009. http://african.lanl.gov/aDORe/ (retrieved April 6, 2009).

American Library Association. *Definition of Digital Preservation,* June 24, 2007. ALCTS Web site. http://www.lita.org/ala/mgrps/divs/alcts/resources/preserv/defdigpres0408.cfm (retrieved April 6, 2009).

Anderson, Chris. "The End of Theory: The Data Deluge Makes the Scientific Method Obsolete." *Wired* 16, no. 7 (June 23, 2008). http://www.wired.com/science/discoveries/magazine/16–07/pb_theory (retrieved April 6, 2009).

Audit Control Environment (ACE). https://wiki.umiacs.umd.edu/adapt/index.php/Ace:Main (retrieved April 6, 2009).

Blue Ribbon Task Force on Sustainable Digital Preservation and Access. *Sustaining the Digital Investment: Issues and Challenges of Economically Sustainable Digital Preservation.* December 2008. http://brtf.sdsc.edu/ (retrieved April 6, 2009).

California Digital Library. http://www.cdlib.org/ (retrieved April 6, 2009).

Caplan, Priscilla. "The Preservation of Digital Materials." *Library Technology Reports* 44, no. 2 (February/March 2008): 26.

Center for Research Libraries. *Digital Archive Reports.* http://www.crl.edu/content.asp?l1=13&l2=58&l3=160 (retrieved April 6, 2009).

Chronopolis. http://chronopolis.sdsc.edu/ (retrieved April 6, 2009).

Dark Archive in the Sunshine State (DAITSS). *DAITSS Overview 1.x,* January 2007. Pdf can be downloaded from http://daitss.fcla.edu/ (retrieved April 6, 2009).

Data Intensive Cyber Environments Group (DICE) Web site. http://diceresearch.org/DICE_Site/Home/Home.html (retrieved April 6, 2009).

DigCCurr. http://ils.unc.edu/digccurr/ (retrieved May 31, 2009).

Digital Preservation Coalition Web site. http://www.dpconline.org/graphics/intro/definitions.html (retrieved April 6, 2009).

DRAMBORA. http://www.repositoryaudit.eu/ (retrieved April 6, 2009).

Florida Digital Archive. *Florida Digital Archive Policy Guide,* August 2007. http://www.fcla.edu/digitalArchive/pdfs/DigitalArchivePolicyGuide.pdf (retrieved April 6, 2009).

Gantz, John F. et al. "The Diverse and Exploding Digital Universe: An Updated Forecast of Worldwide Information Growth through 2011." EMC2, March 2008. http://www.emc.com/collateral/analyst-reports/diverse-exploding-digital-universe.pdf (retrieved April 6, 2009).

Halbert, Martin. *Welcome and Overview of the MetaArchive Cooperative."* October 24, 2008. http://www.metaarchive.org/events/200810_workshop_atl/presentations/MetaArchive-Overview.pdf (retrieved April 6, 2009).

ICPSR. http://www.icpsr.umich.edu/ (retrieved April 6, 2009).

Integrated Rule-Oriented Data System (iRODS) Web site. https://www.irods. org/index.php/IRODS:Data_Grids%2C_Digital_Libraries%2C_Persistent_ Archives%2C_and_Real-time_Data_Systems (retrieved April 6, 2009).

Joint Systems Information Committee. *Digital Preservation Briefing Paper,* 2006. http://www.jisc.ac.uk/publications/publications/pub_digipreservationbp. aspx (retrieved April 6, 2009).

LOCKSS. *Home,* 2009. http://www.lockss.org/lockss/Home (retrieved May 31, 2009).

LOCKSS. *Libraries,* 2009. http://www.lockss.org/lockss/Libraries (retrieved April 6, 2009).

Lots of Copies Keep Stuff Safe (LOCKSS). *How It Works,* 2009. http://www.lockss. org/lockss/How_It_Works (retrieved April 6, 2009).

MetaArchive Cooperative. *About MetaArchive: Collaboratively Preserving our Digital Heritage,* 2009. http://www.metaarchive.org/about.html (retrieved April 6, 2009).

MetaArchive Cooperative. *Current Networks,* 2009. http://www.metaarchive.org/ networks.html (retrieved April 6, 2009).

National Digital Information Infrastructure Preservation Program (NDIIPP). http:// www.digitalpreservation.gov/ (retrieved, April 6, 2009).

NCSU Libraries. http://www.lib.ncsu.edu/ (retrieved April 6, 2009).

Portico. http://www.portico.org/ (retrieved April 6, 2009).

Portico. *About Portico,* 2007. http://www.portico.org/about/ (retrieved April 6, 2009).

Portico. *Service for Libraries,* 2009. http://www.portico.org/libraries/ (retrieved April 6, 2009).

Replication Monitor. https://wiki.umiacs.umd.edu/adapt/index.php/Replication: Main (retrieved April 6, 2009).

Schroeder, Wayne. *Overview of the SDSC Storage Resource Broker,* May 2004. http:// hepwww.rl.ac.uk/hepix/nesc/schroeder.ppt (retrieved April 6, 2009).

Scripps Institution of Oceanography. http://www.sio.ucsd.edu/ (retrieved April 6, 2009).

TRAC. http://www.crl.edu/content.asp?l1=13&l2=58&l3=162&l4=91 (retrieved April 6, 2009).

University of Illinois at Urbana-Champaign Master of Science Specialization in Data Curation. http://www.lis.illinois.edu/programs/ms/data_curation.html (retrieved May 31, 2009).

9

FREE AND OPEN SOURCE SOFTWARE

Scot Colford

VOYAGE OF THE O.S.S. LIBERTY

Think back to when you were six years old and imaginative play was your highest and most serious priority. Your great-aunt Myrtle sends you a generous check to spend on whatever toy you choose, and you have decided that you need a pirate ship with which to discover the sunken treasure at the bottom of your sock drawer. When Father takes you to the toy store you have a plethora of choices, but you are most attracted to colorful ships produced by two manufacturers: Fisher-Price and LEGO.

The Fisher-Price vessel appears quite yare and capable with three simultaneous-launching cannons starboard, sturdy rigging, and a handsomely sized poop deck. However, she has striped sails (which you dislike for aesthetic reasons) permanently affixed to her mainmast, no decorative masthead (and no way to attach one), and a high railing on the crow's nest, which is good for the safety of your crew but ruins the air of danger you were going for. Furthermore, you have doubts about the cannon placement, as the sock drawer is narrow, and it will be difficult to maneuver your ship to tack. Arrgh, me hearty! If only you could reposition them thar cannons to the fo'cs'le!

On the other hand, the LEGO schooner's box doesn't appear to show as large of a poop deck. It also shows striped sails, no masthead, and has cannons installed in scuttles of the starboard hull. Scupper that! It be no better than the first! But, what ho? The LEGO vessel must be built from the parts in the box, while the Fisher-Price ship comes fully assembled. What is more, though the good ship LEGO comes with instructions for how to build the model exactly as displayed on the box, the parts are completely interchangeable because they use a standard button-and-hole bonding system. The cannons can be moved to the fore; the sails can be replaced—you will even be able to use parts of your favorite existing LEGO sets to build just the ship you need. Why, you can borrow your sister's LEGO mermaid for the masthead! You just need to be willing to spend a little time planning and assembling and choosing among the—avast!—865 interlocking pieces. Shiver me timbers!

What will you choose: a fully assembled and configured product that you cannot change or a kit of standard tools that you can alter to build your own customized apparatus? You can get started right away with the former, but you will undoubtedly need to find workarounds for the missing required functionality. Writing the company is also a possibility, hoping that they will include what you need in the next version. (Good luck with that. Expect to pay more for the new version as well.) The ideal product is within your reach with the latter option, but it seems clear that it will take some time to achieve. Not only will you need to build a complex structure from many interdependent pieces, but think of all the time you will spend planning and testing and rebuilding. You can always start with the standard "out-of-the-box" build and alter things slowly from there, but it seems apparent that, at some point, you will need to tackle the major architecture of the product. It may help to find other people who are trying to build similar structures and swap knowledge, but if you find that you just do not have the skills required, you may have to consider hiring someone to build it for you.

Now, most libraries, with the possible exception of public libraries with children's rooms, will not need to put this much thought into toy buying. The differences between the two pirate ships, however, mirror the considerations one makes when choosing between *proprietary* and *open source software* solutions. To end users (in the case above, the end users would be imaginary pirates) there are no functional differences. Well, there certainly *are* functional differences that the end users will notice, but the difference between proprietary and open source applications cannot be determined by these differences alone. The fundamental differences are in what the developer permits others to do with the software and in how the developer builds and distributes the software.

LICENSE TO SHARE

Proprietary software is just that—software that is owned by the proprietor. When you buy Microsoft Office, you are not actually buying a copy of the software. You are buying a CD-ROM, sure. But that is just media. You would not be permitted (or, in most cases, able) to use the program stored on the disc without one important intangible element: a license. Just as a driver's license allows you to operate a motor vehicle, a software license is a legal agreement between you and the entity that owns the software copyright and/or patent that stipulates how you may and may not use the application.

Proprietary software licenses are meant to protect the rights of the copyright holder so they may profit from all of the work and ingenuity that went into designing and programming the application. For this reason, these licenses tend to be more restrictive than permissive. They may be presented in many forms such as paper pamphlets, electronic "clickwrap" (which many people have become accustomed to ignoring completely), or external online documents that must be actively sought out. However the presentation, a proprietary software license may prohibit a user from:

- Reproducing the application, though creating a backup of the installation media may be permitted
- Redistributing, reselling, or giving the license away to others
- Reverse-engineering the software to see how it works or to make changes
- Altering or modifying the software in any way
- Using portions of the application in new software packages (derivative works)
- Installing the software on more computers than specified in the license (licensing per seat)
- Allowing more users to operate the software than specified in the license (licensing per user)
- Using the software for certain fields of endeavor (personal, educational, nonprofit, commercial)
- Publishing the results of performance tests of the software
- Performing many other actions above and beyond what copyright law covers

These restrictions may sound familiar and bring to mind licenses accompanying software distributed by companies such as Microsoft and Apple. But proprietary software is not restricted only to large corporations or even to individuals who hope to reap financial gain from sales. Two alternative types of software licensing are known as *shareware* and *freeware*. These types of licenses do not fall under the open source umbrella. That bears repeating—*by definition, shareware and freeware are not open source*. Shareware refers to a license that allows a user to use a software application for a defined period of time or for a certain number of "launches" before the user must pay for a more permanent license. During the trial period, some actual use restrictions may be enforced, such as limits on how much data may be saved, disabled features, or watermarking of documents, images, video, and so forth created by the program. After the trial period expires, the user may not be able to use the program at all without paying for a license, or the program may continue to operate, simply warning the user that they are in violation of the shareware license upon launch. These warnings are known as *nag screens,* for obvious reasons. Freeware, on the other hand, is software that is accompanied by a proprietary license that is free of cost. You may use freeware without paying for it, but you will still find that there are some restrictions you are legally bound to abide by regarding redistribution, modification, deriving new works, or using the software for unapproved fields of endeavor. Many people confuse "freeware" with "free software," which you will see below, is an entirely different matter.

Open source licensing, however, flips the proprietary licensing paradigm on its head. An open source developer—who may be one person, a corporation, an organized confederation, or a loosely knit group of independent developers—creates software with the express intent of sharing it with others. The license still stipulates what may and may not be done with the application, but rather than restricting the user in what he or she may do with the software, the license grants users a number of freedoms such as the permission to:

- Redistribute the software without paying royalties to the original author
- Examine the software to see how it works and to make any changes desired
- Modify the software and redistribute any derived works
- Obtain a license no matter who he or she is or what the software will be used for (fields of endeavor)

The developer still retains his or her copyright but gives up many of the essential guarantees that right provides. Instead, the open source license restricts users by insisting that they:

- Only redistribute the software or any derived works under the exact same license as the original, essentially ensuring the same freedoms to other users
- Make the source code (the original, uncompiled commands that programmers create) available to anyone who wants it so they may alter the software at will
- Ensure the integrity of the original source code, meaning that if they alter it, they must rename the program or offer modifications as *patches* to the original
- Guarantee that the software they redistribute will not be restricted by a larger, umbrella license for an application the redistribution is incorporated into
- Do not restrict the use of the redistributed software by person, field of endeavor, interface, or technology platform (Open Source Initiative 2006 "Definition")

A WORD ABOUT FREE SOFTWARE

The idea of relinquishing control of software use is not new, relatively speaking. It began before the term "open source" was even coined. In 1977, Richard Stallman, a programmer at MIT, felt that the essential camaraderie of his working group was compromised when mandatory passwords were established for all network accounts at the Lab for Computer Science (*Revolution OS* 2003). It was his feeling that the software being developed should be accessible to all and that the password system was a byproduct of the emergent culture of proprietary licensing. Just the year before, a young Bill Gates had sent an electronic missive to computer hobbyists regarding his perceived exploitation of programmers' output that insisted duplication of software cease (Gates 1976). To counter the imminent operating system monopolies, Stallman initiated the GNU Project in 1984. GNU stands for "GNU's not UNIX," and is an oblique recursive acronym meant to convey that the operating system being developed would not become the same restrictive platform that the proprietary operating system UNIX had become. Stallman's growing discomfort eventually led him to establish the Free Software Foundation (FSF) in 1985.

The Free Software Foundation clearly establishes an ethical (and perhaps moral) guideline regarding the development and distribution of software (Free Software Foundation 2007). "Free software" is a term that Stallman and the FSF use to refer to software that promotes end-user freedom. It does not mean that the software license is free of cost, as the term "freeware" confers. To illustrate his meaning, Stallman likes to describe the discrepancy as such: "'Free software' is a matter of liberty, not price. To understand the concept, you should think of 'free' as in 'free speech,' not as in 'free beer'" (Free Software Foundation 2009).

One of the most common misconceptions about open source software is that it always is distributed free of cost. This confusion can be traced directly back to the first conceptual name of open source software: "free software." Richard Stallman and the FSF now advise that any word that summarizes the concept of "freedom" may be used in place of "free," such as "*libre* software," but the confusion remains in the English language, in part because of the four precepts of free software licensing according to the FSF:

- The freedom to run the program, for any purpose (freedom 0).
- The freedom to study how the program works, and adapt it to your needs (freedom 1). Access to the source code is a precondition for this.
- The freedom to redistribute copies so you can help your neighbor (freedom 2).
- The freedom to improve the program, and release your improvements (and modified versions in general) to the public, so that the whole community benefits (freedom 3). Access to the source code is a precondition for this. (Free Software Foundation 2009)

Note that there is no freedom from cost mentioned, so it is possible for a licensor of free software to charge a fee for the license. In common practice, however, this is rare considering the preconditions of redistribution. Essentially, the concept of free software is one of ethics. All free software is, by definition, open source software, but the reverse is not necessarily so. The line is only important to draw when making a moral, ethical, or political argument.

The most significant event in the history of free software is the publication of the first version of the GNU General Public License (GPL) in 1989. Richard Stallman authored this license to comprehensively ensure the precepts of free software in the distribution of all software developed in the GNU Project. The FSF owns the copyright to the license itself but permits its verbatim redistribution and use (Free Software Foundation 1989). The GPL has undergone two major revisions since 1989 but still outlines the same basic freedoms. Indeed, the genius of this license is in its use of an author's privileges as a copyright holder to insist that the four basic free software freedoms will propagate to all future users of a piece of software through redistribution and derivative works. This unconventional use of copyright has been given its own name by Stallman: *copyleft*.

HOW OPEN SOURCE WORKS

As Stallman and the GNU Project forged ahead, other software developers were arriving at some of the same conclusions regarding the benefits of distributing software with required freedoms attached. The path that led them there was not exactly the same as the one taken by the FSF. Instead, the main advantage cited by many in the 1990s was the ability to have one's work peer reviewed and improved upon, as Eric S. Raymond (2000) vividly exemplifies in his essay, "The Cathedral and the Bazaar." During this decade, a Finnish university student named Linus Torvalds also developed and released a new operating system *kernel* licensed under the GPL (Linux Online 2007). A kernel is a very specific computer program, the nucleus of an operating system that allows all the peripheral programs (known as the *shell*) to interoperate. The combination of this kernel and the programs developed by the GNU Project formed a fully functional free software operating system called Linux. It appealed to many independent software developers in that it very closely resembled UNIX, but users were able to alter and *compile* the kernel to support whatever software they developed. (The process of compiling software turns human-readable programming language into machine code that only a computer can assimilate.) Distinct combinations of the Linux kernel, GNU software, and other free or open source software are called *distributions* and have unique names like Ubuntu, Red Hat Linux, or Debian.

In early 1998, Raymond, Torvalds, and many others conferred about the inherent confusion over the term "free software" and the perceived distastefulness of espousing moral arguments *against* proprietary software in favor of free software. In their view, proprietary software need not be discredited in order to accentuate the benefits of free software. Besides the ingenious concept of copyleft, the main advantage of free software is that the source code is available to other developers who can improve and embellish programs that will stimulate the industry. Because of this, the argument became more one of good business sense than one of principle, so the group decided that they would call such software *open source,* rather than free software. Richard Stallman and the Free Software Foundation briefly contemplated adopting the new term but decided against it. That year, the Open Source Initiative (OSI) was formed with Eric Raymond as its first president, and the organization set about creating its own definition of what constitutes open source software (Open Source Initiative 2006 "History"). The elements enumerated in the definition are very close to the four freedoms defined by the FSF but allow for a little more flexibility in licensing. As a result, one can now claim that a free software program is open source, but not that all open source software is free ("as in liberty"). Given that two organizations exist that promote parallel types of software, it is generally considerate and precise to use the umbrella term "free and open source software" (FOSS or F/OSS) to classify this type of licensing. Many different licenses exist in each category but some of the most commonly used are these:

Table 9.1.

Free software	*Open source software*
• GNU General Public License (GPL)—now updated to version three, though earlier versions are still in use	• Reciprocal Public License—requires that the original developer be notified of derivative works and that all derivatives be made publicly available
• GNU Lesser General Public License (LGPL)—similar to the GPL but allows derivative works to interoperate with nonfree software, whereas the GPL does not	• OCLC Research Public License—allows for distributions of nonmodifiable code
• Apache License—developed for the popular web server Apache	• PHP License—also a free software license, but only grudgingly, since it places restrictions on the use of the term "PHP" in derivative works
• FreeBSD license—a modified version of the original BSD license, which was developed by the University of California, Berkeley	• Essentially, all the other licenses deemed to be free software
• X11 License—sometimes called the "MIT License"	
• Mozilla Public License (MPL)	

(Free Software Foundation, 2009; Open Source Initiative 2006 "Definition")

DON'T LOOK NOW, BUT YOUR SOURCE IS OPEN

While knowing the history and philosophy that stimulated the development of F/OSS is an essential part of understanding its usefulness, the complex developer-centered narrative can leave one with a sense that F/OSS requires a degree in computer science (or at the very least, a deep knowledge of classic Star Trek episodes and comic books) to make use of it. This misapprehension can be easily rectified, however.

Consider your last dinner party. If you are a busy professional and have scheduled a dinner for eight on a Friday night, you might opt to feed your guests by stopping by your local grocery store on your way home and picking up some Caterer's Choice frozen crab rangoons, a bag of Dole "Fresh Discoveries" premixed salad, a couple boxes of Green Giant frozen green bean casserole, and a Sara Lee cheesecake. After a stop at Boston Market for a couple rotisserie chickens, all you have to do to prepare is to heat it all up, arrange it all artfully, and hide the original containers to be complimented on a delicious meal. This would be a proprietary solution to your dilemma. You might even decide to have the groceries delivered for an extra fee, resolving some of your installation … er, preparation concerns.

Another option might be to take a day (or two) off work and prepare everything yourself from scratch. Any cook knows that "from scratch" is a subjective term, however. Is your casserole made from loose green beans bought from a farm stand or did you pick them from your garden? Do you use canned, condensed mushroom soup or do you make a sauce from flour, butter, cream, and fresh mushrooms? For that matter, do you use the recipe that Tyler Florence shared on Food Network, or do you experiment and "wing it" yourself? This is an open source solution because you are using the source elements that make up the complete application … er, meal that you will serve your guests. You don't know precisely how to recreate Green Giant green bean casserole, but you can achieve the same result. And as an added plus, you know exactly what went into it and can personalize it with some experimentation and extra effort.

There are other choices as well. You may decide to hire a caterer to create a homemade meal for you and deliver it. This is akin to hiring a vendor to install and manage your open source solution. You may con your best friend into cooking the meal if he or she is a gourmet chef, which is the same as using in-house technical staff to develop your solution. Or, if you are like many home chefs, you'll think about the suitability of each prepared item that you can buy and decide if a homemade version will better satisfy your guests. For example, Sara Lee may be perfectly appropriate for you to eat alone at midnight, but only a cheesecake made with love will make your party successful—even if the person supplying the love is your neighborhood baker. This is a *hybrid* solution.

If you followed the analogy, you may already realize that many libraries *already use* a hybrid solution when using technology to serve patrons and/

Table 9.2.

Commonly used open source applications

• Operating systems
  ○ GNU/Linux
  ○ FreeBSD/OpenBSD
	• Web and proxy servers
	  ○ Apache
	  ○ Squid cache

• Web browsers
  ○ Firefox
  ○ Lynx
	• Blogs
	  ○ WordPress
	  ○ Movable Type

• Office software
  ○ OpenOffice.org
  ○ PDFCreator
	• Wikis
	  ○ MediaWiki
	  ○ TikiWiki

• Instant messengers
  ○ Gaim
  ○ Pidgin
	• Content management systems
	  ○ Drupal
	  ○ Joomla

or staff and have done so for many years. Librarians of a certain age may remember (fondly, even) text-based PINE e-mail. A library that hosted PINE on a UNIX server was running an open source application on a proprietary operating system. Today, one librarian may use Mozilla Thunderbird (open source) to access e-mail, while another staff member in the same library uses Microsoft Outlook (proprietary) instead. Similarly, Microsoft Internet Explorer (IE) and Firefox are frequently installed on many librarians' computers. IE is entirely proprietary, but Firefox, though released under that name as a proprietary application, is built on the open source Mozilla engine. Anyone is free to download the source code behind Firefox and redistribute it—as long as they don't use the Firefox name or logo. ("We've secretly replaced this fresh ground coffee with Folger's Crystals. Will it be rich enough?") Proprietary vendor-supplied integrated library systems like SirsiDynix Unicorn or Symphony may be hosted on F/OSS server operating systems like Linux. Open source web applications like MediaWiki or WordPress can be installed on a Microsoft Windows server, provided that PHP (the open source hypertext preprocessor engine that parses the application scripts) is also installed. If any of these environments sound familiar to you, though you thought open source software to be strange or exotic, expect your manicurist to inform you that "You're soaking in it!" at your next appointment. If they are unfamiliar, have a conversation with your IT staff. You may be surprised at the open source software that facilitates your daily work.

WHAT'S THE BIG DEAL?

If F/OSS applications are already pervasive in library technological environments, then why is such a fuss being made over the topic now? The answer, like the answer to so many quandaries faced by libraries, deals with

conventional practice, complacency, and a resistance to change. It also, paradoxically, involves libraries' need to adopt information storage and retrieval
technology earlier than other organizations. By the time the Free Software
Foundation was established in 1985, library automation vendors (which are
now known as ILS vendors) had established a de facto proprietary licensing
model for automation software such as CARL, DRA, Aleph, GEAC, and
NOTIS (Breeding 2007). Ironically, 1985 was also the year that Virginia
Tech Library Systems (VTLS) incorporated as a for-profit company in order
to sell the automation product developed for Virginia Tech (VTLS 2008).
By the time "open source" was coined as a term and the benefit of using
F/OSS software to achieve business goals was taking root in 1998, almost
every library in the United States had established a firm investment in one
automation vendor or another. Anyone who has been involved in a migration between such vendors knows that it is a costly, lengthy, and taxing process that is not to be undertaken indiscriminately. As a result, many libraries
stayed with the same proprietary vendor and product for years until the software neared *end of life* (meaning that development had ceased and vendor
support was limited) or beyond. When migrating to a new vendor, or to a
new product from the *same* vendor (given that by 2001 many companies had
been acquired by others, a trend that has only increased since then), libraries
had fewer available choices.

The products on the market at the turn of the century promised to address all automation needs libraries faced, but each integrated library system
did so in its own way. Of course, user groups were formed by users of many
major ILS vendor products, but the process of submitting enhancement requests to the vendor frustrated many customers. This development cycle,
still widespread today among proprietary ILS vendors, attempts to address
concerns and requests common among all libraries using the software, but it
is problematic in many ways. First, if a small minority of libraries requires an
absolutely critical change, the enhancement request is unlikely to be passed
on to the vendor. ("Just live with it.") Second, so many libraries of different
types and missions exist that it is often difficult to agree upon a preferred set
of functionality. ("One size does not fit all.") Third, the enhancement requests that a user group *can* come to agreement on tend to pertain either to
glaringly obvious bugs that should already be at the top of the vendor's list,
or they regard such insignificantly trivial modifications that the energy put
into generating the enhancement request list is wasted. ("Banging your head
against a wall.") And fourth, an enhancement request list is just that: a list
of *requests*. A request will only be fulfilled by a commercial vendor if it makes
good business sense to do so. ("Thank you for your input.")

Over the years, thousands of industrious systems librarians have made val-
iant efforts to overcome the native shortcomings of different ILSs and have
striven to work around undesirable functionality in them. These librarians
have contributed countless hours in service to their libraries and patrons, but

it is only at user group meetings or on community electronic mailing lists that they can pass on what they have learned and invented. Beyond these outlets, their work is largely performed in isolation, and dozens of people often create slightly passable workarounds to identical problems without having access to the original application source code.

In 2005, the Georgia Public Library Service came to the end of its search for a proprietary replacement for the Sirsi Unicorn ILS they had been using. Unicorn was rapidly proving itself inadequate for the needs of its automated lending consortium PINES, comprised of more than 250 libraries of various types. All of the options available on the commercial market had been deemed unable to meet the requirements of the particularly large consortium. Rather than making do with one of the major vendors, the statewide agency decided instead to develop their ILS in-house (Georgia Public Library Service 2009). The resulting ILS, Evergreen, was released the next year and is specifically designed to handle the needs of large consortia. Since then, many other libraries have dedicated developer staff time to help improve Evergreen, and other successful installations have been launched at the Michigan Library Consortium (http://www.mlcnet.org/evergreen/) and the British Columbia public library consortium SITKA (http://sitka.bclibraries.ca/). Other library systems have major migration projects in progress, including King County Library System (http://www.kcls.org/) and Project Conifer (http://conifer.mcmaster.ca/), a collaboration of five academic libraries in Ontario, Canada. Evergreen was not the first widely distributed open source ILS, however.

In New Zealand, the Horowhenua Library Trust (HLT) faced a similarly trying experience in 1999 when they were forced to plan for a replacement of their end-of-life ILS. But rather than finding proprietary solutions lacking in technological or design advances, HLT (a small district library system with four branches within 20 miles of each other) decided that the commercial solution maintenance costs were too pricey. The required telecommunications upgrades, in particular, were too overwhelming for the system to contemplate, given that the branches were still using dialup network connections. After talks with Katipo Communications, a web development firm, HLT decided to contract out the development of an ILS created just for them. After six years, Katipo deployed the first version of Koha at HLT (Koha Development Team & LibLime 2008). Since then, developers from all over the globe have contributed to Koha and in 2008 version three was released.

Both Evergreen and Koha are licensed as open source and may be freely downloaded from the Web. In keeping with the open source and free software definitions, the current source code is also available for customization and redistribution under the terms of the GNU General Public License. A library need not employ a software developer (or a team of them) in order to obtain a custom ILS, though. The software team that initially developed Evergreen founded the company Equinox in 2006 to coordinate continued development of the software and now "sells various services to libraries implementing Evergreen: data migration from legacy systems, training, support, and specialized development" (Equinox, Inc. 2008). Similarly, the Athens, Ohio, consulting company LibLime was founded in 2005 to consult with libraries on the implementation of open source software solutions. Later that year, LibLime partnered with Katipo Communications to manage development of Koha, and, today, LibLime has fully absorbed that responsibility (LibLime 2008). The assimilation of Equinox and LibLime into the landscape of proprietary ILS vendors has been confusing to many in the library profession. Marshall Breeding, who maintains the Web site Library Technology Guides (http://www.librarytechnology.org), includes them both in his continual analysis of ILS vendors as if they were the sole source of Evergreen and Koha licensing and support. However, both companies function as consultants that can assist libraries without appropriate internal staffing to install, maintain, and develop open source ILSs. Additionally, unlike the enhancement system of major proprietary vendors, the custom development these companies are able to perform goes straight back into the product that is freely customizable by libraries that do not contract with either LibLime or Equinox.

One need not have a heart transplant to improve one's circulation, and a library need not replace its ILS to achieve the same goal. How about a jog around the block with a smaller-scale application? As the library community became frustrated with the fewer commercial choices available and their sizeable required investments in a broad range of library services, vendors began to get the message and added modular mix-and-match elements or add-ons that libraries could choose from. The hope was to retain current ILS customers while gaining more who appreciate the function of, say, an OPAC developed by someone other than their main ILS vendor. Federated search, link resolver, and digital repository packages could also be licensed as third-party applications, opening the door to even more customers and revenue. As these developments are more recent, however, many libraries and library developers began to create their *own* open source versions of these tools. Digital and institutional repository software development, in particular, flourishes in the open source licensing model, as it is dependent upon common standards for data ingestion and exchange. For this reason, DSpace and Fedora have set the bar for digital asset storage and retrieval. OPACs, on the other hand, need to interface with an existing ILS, but once this hurdle is cleared there are a wealth of open source tools that can truly modernize the user interface such as seen in SOPAC, the social OPAC, and Scriblio, which is based on Word-Press. Both of these OPACs can be used as the only portal to a library's bibliographic holdings or either can be used as an alternate interface containing the value added features common on social networks, such as comments, ratings, reviews, and faceted searching. At any rate, these smaller projects allow libraries to dip a virtual toe into the waters of F/OSS with less fear of failure.

Table 9.3.

Open source library applications

- ILSs
  - Evergreen
  - Koha
- Digital repositories
  - Digital Asset Factory
  - DSpace
  - Fedora
- Metasearch/Resolvers
  - CUFTS
  - LibraryFind
  - VuFind

- OPACs
  - Blacklight
  - Kochief (formerly Fac-Back-OPAC)
  - MARC Module for Drupal
  - Scriblio
  - SOPAC

MAKING THE CASE FOR F/OSS

In her keynote speech at the 2007 Code4Lib conference in Athens, Georgia, Karen Schneider (then Associate Director for Libraries and Technology at Florida State University, but now Community Librarian for Equinox, Inc.) presented a lighthearted, yet deadly accurate list of "what [library] directors 'know' about open source." They know that open source software is developed and maintained by "one guy in a garage … probably in a torn Duran Duran tee-shirt." In other words, the prevailing belief is that open source is equivalent to *hacking,* and while software developers will claim that the term "hacking" refers to the development of clever solutions to difficult problems, news reports of security breaches, computer viruses, and identity theft plant an entirely different image in the minds of nontechnical professionals. Furthermore, Schneider thinks this image of the lone hacker presents a fear of a haphazard model support, if any: "One car accident away from orphan software," in fact. The hacker scenario also brings to mind "cheesy, make-do quality" and software that is "arcane and developer-oriented," according to Schneider. Given the history of free and open source software, this last belief is easy to embrace. Developers *do* speak their own language, but as has been illustrated above, many F/OSS applications have already been adopted by laypeople, often without any awareness of the licensing or the oblique benefits attached. Lastly, Schneider claims that directors "know" that if they undertook an open source project, their library would be entirely on their own because "no one else is doing it." In fact, the opposite is true. Two of the greatest strengths of F/OSS are the community of developers and users with whom one may communicate and the open standards upon which the software is based. Proprietary vendors may have many more customers than a F/OSS application has users, but those customers will have little opportunity or ability to help themselves or each other in any significant way. One additional, and completely contrary, belief that many directors hold is that open source means free—"free as in free beer," not "free as in liberty." While this misconception can fire a short-term enthusiasm in those who hold the purse strings, it can be quite dangerous to encourage. Schneider, who happens to be a beer home- brewing enthusiast, surely refers to "free as in free beer" when she asserts, "There is no such thing as free software," and, monetarily speaking, this is absolutely true. A F/OSS deployment will cost money, whether it is in staff time, consultant fees, or lost productivity due to a poorly planned implementation by under-qualified staff.

The result of these common misconceptions combined with a librarian's enthusiasm for open source can be unpredictable, so Schneider offers some ironic advice. Do not use the words "open source" to your director, your trustees, your administrative council, or your patrons when pointing out the value of an application. Instead, compare the features of proprietary and F/OSS solutions. Weigh the costs and benefits: upfront, recurring, immediate, long-term, tangible, and intangible. Present them in a side-by-side comparison and if a question comes up about open source, simply use what you have learned here to correct false impressions. But whatever you do, make sure not to use "because it is open source" as an argument.

REFERENCES

Breeding, Marshall. "History of Library Automation," *Library Technology Guides*, 2007. http://www.librarytechnology.org/automationhistory.pl?SID=2009071 3242034912 (accessed April 24, 2009).

Equinox Software, Inc. "Equinox Software Company History," 2008. http://www. esilibrary.com/esi/company.php (accessed April 24, 2009).

Free Software Foundation. "GNU General Public License Version 1," February 1989. http://www.gnu.org/licenses/old-licenses/gpl-1.0.txt (accessed April 24, 2009).

Free Software Foundation. "iPhone Restricts Users, GPLv3 Frees Them," June 28, 2007. http://www.fsf.org/iphone-gplv3/view (accessed April 24, 2009).

Free Software Foundation. "The Free Software Definition," January 8, 2009. http://www.fsf.org/licensing/essays/free-sw.html (accessed April 24, 2009).

Gates, Bill. "An Open Letter to Hobbyists," *The History of Microsoft*, 1976. http://www.microsoft.com/about/companyinformation/timeline/timeline/docs/di_Hobbyists.doc (accessed April 24, 2009).

Georgia Public Library Service. "Evergreen_faq_1," *Evergreen DokuWiki*, March 25, 2009. http://www.open-ils.org/dokuwiki/doku.php?id=faqs:evergreen_faq_1 (accessed April 24, 2009).

Koha Development Team & LibLime. "Horowhenua Library Trust," 2008. http://www.koha.org/about-koha/case-studies/hlt.html (accessed April 24, 2009).

LibLime. 2008. http://www.liblime.com (accessed April 24, 2009).

Linux Online. "Linus Torvalds Bio," September 7, 2007. http://www.linux.org/info/linus.html (accessed April 24, 2009).

Open Source Initiative. "History of the OSI," September 19, 2006. http://www.opensource.org/history (accessed April 24, 2009).

Open Source Initiative. "The Open Source Definition," July 7, 2006. http://www. opensource.org/docs/osd (accessed April 24, 2009).

Raymond, Eric S. "The Cathedral and the Bazaar," 2000. http://www.catb.org/~esr/ writings/cathedral-bazaar/cathedral-bazaar/ (accessed April 24, 2009).

Revolution OS, DVD, directed by J.T.S. Moore (2002; Los Angeles, CA: Wonderview Productions, 2003).

Schneider, Karen G. "Hurry Up Please It's Time." Keynote speech presented at the 2007 Code4Lib Conference, The University of Georgia, Athens, GA, February 28–March 2, 2007.

VTLS, Inc. "Vinod Chachra, PhD, President & CEO," VTLS, 2008. http://www. vtls.com/about/management/bio/VinodChachra (accessed April 24, 2009).

10

METADATA REPURPOSING USING XSLT

Maureen P. Walsh

With the current proliferation of heterogeneous digital resources and the metadata schemas[1] used to describe them, librarians are faced with ever-new challenges in providing information to users. With the ubiquity of XML[2] in today's information environment, coupled with its ability to act as common denominator for all types of metadata, librarians are also presented with ever-increasing opportunities to meet user needs. To respond to the challenges and take advantage of the opportunities, the metadata environment has seen a shift from metadata creation to the optimized use of the many varieties and sources of metadata available for resource discovery over distributed collections. XML has greatly enhanced the potential for interoperable[3] systems and schemas in terms of the exchange of structured data, or metadata, between them. Work continues to be done to develop interoperability standards and best practices, and to improve semantic interoperability, or the exchange of data meaning and relationships. New resource discovery tools and systems are taking advantage of the interoperability XML affords, and metadata is increasingly used in new and different ways other than what was originally intended at creation. A very common way to reuse library metadata is to convert it for a new purpose using XSLT,[4] a transformation language written in XML.

INTRODUCTION TO XSLT

XSLT is a member of the Extensible Stylesheet Language Family (XSL).[5] The XSL family is made up of XSL Transformations (XSLT), XML Path

Language (XPath)[6] and XSL Formatting Objects (XSL-FO).[7] The three parts of XSL are used for defining XML document transformation and presentation. XSLT is a markup language for transforming XML documents. XPath is a text-based language for navigating in XML documents and is used with XSLT to select the parts of XML to process. XSL-FO is a markup language for formatting XML data and describes how the source content is displayed (laid out and paginated) in print. XSL-FO is most often used for output to Adobe's Portable Document Format (PDF) or Postscript. XSL-FO is not needed to perform transformations in XSLT and will not be covered in this chapter.

There are currently two versions of XSL Transformations, XSLT 1.0 and XSLT 2.0. This is also true of XPath. The first versions of XSLT and XPath became World Wide Web Consortium (W3C) recommendations in November 1999. XSLT 2.0 and XPath 2.0 became W3C recommendations in January 2007, and together they include new functionality for grouping and string manipulation as well as support for datatypes, XML schema, and regular expressions. XSLT 2.0 and XPath 2.0 retain a high level of backward compatibility, and many library applications of XSLT continue to use XSLT 1.0 and XPath 1.0.

XML documents written in XSLT are commonly referred to as stylesheets. These stylesheets can transform source XML documents into a variety of formats, including XHTML, HTML, PDFs, text, and new XML documents. Although it is common to use XLST to transform XML into XHTML and HTML for the Web, this chapter will only cover the transformation of XML into new XML.

XSLT is a very functional tool for non-IT librarians. XSLT is powerful and flexible, but it is also a relatively simple language for working with XML that does not require programming experience or coding with Java, Visual Basic, Perl, or Python to be able to transform XML documents. For librarians who have a basic understanding of XML it has a low learning curve for common library metadata applications. XSLT can be viewed in all major browsers and can be written and edited in plain text editors, such as the Windows text editor, Notepad. However, an XSLT processor, or engine, is needed to make use of XSLT's ability to transform XML. As diagrammed in figure 10.1, the source XML document and an XSLT stylesheet are input to an XSLT processor and a new output results, in this case a new XML document. Many of the XML editors available today, including XMLSpy[8] and <oXygen/>,[9] support both XSLT 1.0 and XSLT 2.0 and also include XSLT debuggers and processors. Stand-alone processors can also be used to run XSLT, including MSXSL,[10] Saxon,[11] and Xalan.[12] An excellent low-barrier XSLT processing tool is included in the freely available MarcEdit[13] software developed by Terry Reese.

It is far beyond the scope of this chapter to provide a full explanation of XSLT. There are many XSLT how-to manuals on the market that take you

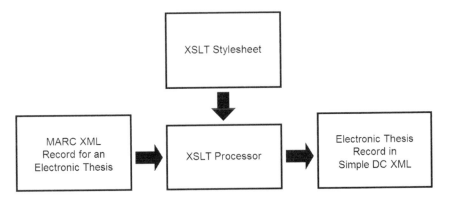

Figure 10.1.

step-by-step through the language and as many that can be used for quick reference for particular questions or to solve particular problems. Instead, after presenting the basics of transforming an XML document with XSLT, this chapter focuses on particular uses of XSLT geared toward non-IT librarians. Librarians interested in working with metadata in new ways and manipulating metadata for new purposes can begin to explore the uses of XSLT data transformations for XML metadata without the prerequisite of a comprehensive knowledge of XSLT. The jump-right-in approach is helped tremendously by the stylesheets freely available with the MarcEdit software and from the Library of Congress Web site.[14] The stylesheets that MarcEdit and the Library of Congress provide can be used as out-of-the-box stylesheets, as the basis for local modifications, or as examples and guides for librarians to write their own.

THE BASICS OF TRANSFORMING AN XML DOCUMENT WITH XSLT

When writing an XSLT stylesheet to transform an XML document you are essentially providing an example of the changes you would like to see. Although XML is human readable, XSLT processors don't read through a stylesheet line by line. XSLT processors look at the information in an XML document as a tree structure with a defined hierarchy. XSLT processors navigate the branches of this tree called nodes looking for the information the XPath expressions in the stylesheet define. The new information structure of the output document is defined by template rules. XSLT processors look for template rule matches to determine the nodes to process and in what order to process them.

XSLT stylesheets are usually written to make changes to batches of records at one time. For example, a library may batch process a set of records received from a publisher in the ONIX[15] format to convert it to

MARCXML.[16] A series of XSLT stylesheets can also be used to make itera-
tive changes to a set of records. A library can convert the format of a set of
records with one stylesheet and then process those new records with one or
more different stylesheets designed to clean up the quality of the metadata.
At this point it would be instructive to show an example of changing just
one MARC[17] record and to focus on just one field in that record, the title
field. For this example we have a physical book and a new digitized version
of the book. The physical book was previously cataloged and has a MARC
record in the library catalog. We want to add the electronic version of the
book to our digital repository, but we do not want to have to recatalog, or
rekey, the descriptive metadata that was already created for the physical item
in the library catalog. The following is a micro illustration of the steps we
would take to repurpose the library catalog metadata for use in the digital
repository.

Step I—Extract the MARC record data from the library catalog

Most of us are familiar with looking at MARC data formatted for display or editing, but to reuse the MARC data we will need to extract the raw
MARC from the library catalog. Box 10.1 shows the example book record
in MARC formatted for display. Box 10.2 shows the same book record in
raw MARC. The title field we will be concentrating on is highlighted in both
figures. Methods of extracting the raw MARC vary depending on the cataloging system used. If we were using the Innovative Interfaces Millennium[18]
product, we would use the data exchange function to output the MARC
data to our PC.

```
     LEADER 00000nam 2200000 a 4500
     001   21670808
     003   OCoLC
     005   19930506085605.0
     008   900516s1990   ohu    b  s001 0 eng
     010   90-7534
     020   0814205305 (alk. paper)
     035   5263745
     040   DLC|cDLC|dOSU
     090   PS3545.A748|bZ8 R79 1990
     090 00 PS3545.A748|bZ8 R79 1990
     100 1  Runyon, Randolph,|d1947-
     245 14 The taciturn text :|bthe fiction of Robert Penn Warren /
            |cRandolph Paul Runyon
     260   Columbus :|bOhio State University Press,|cc1990
     300   ix, 288 p. ;|c24 cm
     504   Includes bibliographical references (p. 279-283) and index
     600 10 Warren, Robert Penn,|d1905-1989|xFictional works
```

Box 10.1.

```
01135nam 2200289 a
45000010012000000030006000120050017000180080041000350100012000760200002
80008803500350011603500120015104000180016309000290018109000290021010000
02900239245008400268260005300352300002500040550400640043060000500049499
80048005449100014005929400043006069450098006499450098007470-ocm21670808
-OCoLC-19930506085605.0-900516s1990  ohu     b  s001 0 eng  -  a90-7534-  -
a0814205305 (alk. paper)-  a.b2620051xb04-07-06c04-21-94-  a5263745-  aDLCcDLC-
dOSU-  aPS3545.A748bZ8  R79 1990-00aPS3545.A748bZ8  R79 1990-1 aRunyon,
Randolph,d1947--14aThe tacitum text :bthe fiction of Robert Penn Warren /cRandolph
Paul Runyon.-  aColumbus :bOhio State University Press,cc1990.-  aix, 288 p. ;c24 cm.-
aIncludes bibliographical references (p. 279-283) and index.-10aWarren, Robert Penn,-
d1905-xFictional works.
```

Box 10.2.

Step 2—Change the MARC Data Format to MARCXML

XSLT requires that the source document be in XML. Our example source record we extracted from the catalog is in MARC. The next step in repurposing this MARC metadata for use in a digital repository is to transform it to MARCXML. The Library of Congress has an XSLT stylesheet tool for converting MARC to MARCXML, called the MARCXML Toolkit, available on their Web site.[19] For this exercise I used the MARC to MARCXML conversion tool built into the MarcEdit software. Box 10.3 shows an extract of the result of the conversion of the book record into MARCXML and highlights the title field.

Step 3—Change the MARCXML to Dublin Core Format

To be able to ingest our book record into our digital repository we will need to convert the MARCXML to the metadata format the repository uses. In this example the repository format is Simple Dublin Core.[20] To change our record format from MARCXML to Simple Dublin Core we will need an XSLT stylesheet written for this conversion. A complete stylesheet for converting MARCXML to Simple Dublin Core is available to view on the Web via the Library of Congress Web site.[21] For this example I have used the MARC21slim (MARCXML) to OAI (Simple) Dublin Core stylesheet and XSLT processor included with the MarcEdit software. Box 10.4 shows the portion of the stylesheet for converting the field we are concentrating on, the title field. Of particular note in this portion of the stylesheet are the highlighted subfield codes the stylesheet is asking for. Only the listed subfields will be converted for output. You will notice that "c," or the subfield for the statement of responsibility in a title field, is not listed. By not including

```
<?xml version="1.0" encoding="UTF-8" ?>
<marc:collection xmlns:marc="http://www.loc.gov/MARC21/slim"
xmlns:xsi="http://www.w3.org/2001/XMLSchema-instance"
xsi:schemaLocation="http://www.loc.gov/MARC21/slim
http://www.loc.gov/standards/marcxml/schema/MARC21slim.xsd">
<marc:record><marc:leader>01135nam a2200289 a 4500</marc:leader>
<marc:controlfield tag="001">ocm21670808</marc:controlfield>
[...section ommitted]
<marc:datafield tag="100" ind1="1" ind2=" ">
<marc:subfield code="a">Runyon, Randolph,</marc:subfield>
<marc:subfield code="d">1947-</marc:subfield>
</marc:datafield>
<marc:datafield tag="245" ind1="1" ind2="4">
<marc:subfield code="a">The taciturn text :</marc:subfield>
<marc:subfield code="b">the fiction of Robert Penn Warren /</marc:subfield>
<marc:subfield code="c">Randolph Paul Runyon.</marc:subfield>
</marc:datafield>
<marc:datafield tag="260" ind1=" " ind2=" ">
<marc:subfield code="a">Columbus :</marc:subfield>
<marc:subfield code="b">Ohio State University Press,</marc:subfield>
<marc:subfield code="c">c1990.</marc:subfield>
</marc:datafield>
[...section ommitted]
</marc:record>
</marc:collection>
```

Box 10.3.

subfield code "c" the statement of responsibility will be excluded from the resulting title-field output in Simple Dublin Core. Box 10.5 shows the resulting Simple Dublin Core record for the book with the title field highlighted. This example illustrates a basic repurposing scenario. In reality, we would most likely customize the generic XSLT stylesheet for the output we desired for our digital repository.

So far this chapter has briefly enumerated the basic functioning of XSLT as a tool to convert metadata formats. We have seen that metadata schemas sharing a common markup language, XML, greatly enhance the syntactic and structural interoperability of cross-domain metadata schemas. However, the real heavy lifting in repurposing metadata is the intellectual work involved in transforming heterogeneous metadata schemas. Before a metadata schema can be converted to a different schema a map needs to be created to bridge the two schemas. The metadata map is the intellectual power behind the XSLT stylesheet used to transform one metadata schema to another.

```
<xsl:for-each select="marc:datafield[@tag=245]">

  <dc:title>

    <xsl:call-template name="subfieldSelect">

      <xsl:with-param name="codes">abfghk</xsl:with-param>

    </xsl:call-template>

  </dc:title>

</xsl:for-each>
```

Box 10.4.

```
<?xml version="1.0" encoding="UTF-8" ?>
<oai_dc:dc xsi:schemaLocation="http://www.openarchives.org/OAI/2.0/oai_dc/
http://www.openarchives.org/OAI/2.0/oai_dc.xsd" xmlns:oai_dc="http://
www.openarchives.org/OAI/2.0/oai_dc/" xmlns:xsi="http://www.w3.org/2001/
XMLSchema-instance" xmlns:dc="http://purl.org/dc/elements/1.1/">
<dc:title>The taciturn text : the fiction of Robert Penn Warren /</dc:title>
<dc:creator> Runyon, Randolph, 1947- </dc:creator>
<dc:type>text</dc:type>
<dc:publisher>Columbus : Ohio State University Press,</dc:publisher>
<dc:date>c1990.</dc:date>
<dc:language>eng</dc:language>
<dc:description>Includes bibliographical references (p. 279-283) and index.</dc:description>
<dc:subject>Warren, Robert Penn, 1905-</dc:subject>
</oai_dc:dc>
```

Box 10.5.

METADATA MAPPING AND CROSSWALKS

Repurposing metadata requires both mapping and crosswalks. For the purposes of this chapter *mapping* refers to the process of establishing semantic relationships between metadata schemas, and *maps*, or *crosswalks*, are the visual representations of mapping. To be able to transform metadata in one schema to a different schema the intellectual work of figuring out how the two schemas relate to each other must be done. In comparing two different metadata schemas the goal is to find relationships and equivalences. A crosswalk strives to find correlations between elements that have the same or similar meanings. The semantic mapping of elements is not always easy to achieve. The elements in different metadata schemas rarely have a one-to-one relationship. In cases where exact matches are not possible, a correspondence in how each metadata schema encodes a shared understanding of meanings is looked for. Given the differing levels of complexity and granularity, or detail, in metadata schemas, mapping often exhibits some degree of incompatibility where elements are not entirely expressed or simply left out.

Table 10.1 shows a portion of a MARC to Dublin Core crosswalk. It also shows on a microscale the inherent differences in granularity that exist when comparing one schema to another. A crosswalk between MARC and Dublin Core demonstrates multiple many-to-one relationships. MARC is a very rich and complex metadata schema. By comparison, Dublin Core is a simpler schema. When mapping MARC to Dublin Core, the granularity, or level of detail in MARC, is lost.

Semantic interoperability between heterogeneous metadata schemas is supported by semantic mapping. The ability to search differently described resources from multiple domains effectively depends upon a common understanding of what the descriptions mean. Semantic interoperability allows the exchange of meaningful information between systems and applications. In addition to the problems of granularity and incompatible descriptions between metadata schemas, semantic mapping is complicated by external relationships not directly expressed in metadata schemas. Content standards are one such relationship. The value of the data contained in metadata elements is often formulated according to rules external to the schema. Examples of different content standards include multiple subject thesauri, name authority files, and descriptive cataloging rules. The ability to search effectively is hampered when metadata following different rules is brought together. To illustrate, two metadata schemas may each have an author element or field that can be mapped with a one-to-one relationship. However, the form of the data value in that field, the author name, may be entered very differently depending on the rules the metadata schema follows. For example, one schema may use the Library of Congress Name Authority File and the other the Getty Union List of Artist Names. It is also common with Web-enabled metadata schemas that the author field is not controlled and any form is allowed. While crosswalks have successfully mapped data structures, there is work to be done to be able to map data values effectively.

Table 10.1.

MARC Fields	Dublin Core Elements
130, 240, 245, 246	Title
100, 110, 111	Creator
700, 710, 711	Contributor
600, 610, 630, 650, 651, 653	Subject
008/07-10 260 $c	Date

Successful schema mapping for repurposing metadata requires knowledge of the data structures and the transformation language being used as well as an intimate knowledge of each metadata schema. Librarians who have a thorough knowledge of the metadata schemas they work with, both syntactically and semantically, are of great advantage to metadata repurposing projects. There are many ways in which libraries can take advantage of XSLT transformations to repurpose metadata. Two possible scenarios for reusing metadata are outlined in the following section.

REPURPOSING METADATA: XSLT USE CASES

XSLT is a useful tool to be aware of when working toward improving resource discovery and access for end users. In addition to Dublin Core, libraries are increasingly using emerging XML based standards such as METS,[22] MODS,[23] PREMIS,[24] and MIX[25] to manage and provide access to their digital library resources. In many cases libraries have preexisting metadata in legacy formats, and in lieu of rekeying that data, are transforming their legacy data to emerging standards to take advantage of what they have to offer for interoperability, preservation, and display. There are many current and potential applications for XSLT in the areas of metadata management, metadata migration, metadata quality control, and delivering metadata to the Web in today's digital environment. The following use cases outline just two of the ways librarians can use XSLT to repurpose metadata.

XSLT Use Case One: Legacy Metadata

For most libraries, the vast majority of metadata the library has is in the MARC format. Over the years, tremendous amounts of time and energy have gone into the creation and maintenance of this treasure trove of homogenous descriptive data. With the increasing prominence of digital resources many libraries are transitioning to Web-enabled non-MARC metadata for their digital collections to meet the needs of today's users. In this environment of mixed MARC and non-MARC metadata, the data in the MARC format is often considered legacy data.

Repurposing legacy metadata can be done on either a large or small scale. A large scale scenario may come into play with the possible implementation of RDA[26] and a subsequent migration away from the MARC format. Projects on a smaller scale can include providing improved Web access to library special collections described in MARC. The following will describe such a scenario.

Objective

The library has a collection of oral history audio tapes and transcripts that are cataloged in MARC. The library has digitized both the audio tapes and the transcripts and wants to provide access to them via their digital repository without having to recatalog the material. The digital repository uses Qualified Dublin Core.

Method

Step One: Output the MARC data for the collection from the library catalog to the desktop. Some libraries have a script for doing this; other libraries rely on the library system function for outputting data. In this scenario III's Millennium create list and data exchange functions are used. The MARC records are gathered in a list based on distinguishing data for the collection and data exchange is used to output the MARC records file to the PC.

Step Two: Convert the MARC data output to MARCXML. In this scenario MarcEdit will be used. The MARC to MARC21XML stylesheet/function is used and the MARC output file from the library catalog is the input file for the transform. A file of MARCXML records is output from MarcEdit.

Step Three: Determine the relationship between the existing metadata used to describe the physical collection and the description that will be necessary for the digital collection. Using an existing MARC to Qualified Dublin Core crosswalk, modify the map to accommodate local variations and desired outcome.

Step Four: Create a customized XSLT stylesheet to convert the MARCXML metadata to Qualified Dublin Core as represented by the mapping previously created. The MARC21slim (MARCXML) to OAI (Simple) Dublin Core stylesheet included with the MarcEdit software is used as a template. This stylesheet is modified to be used for Qualified Dublin Core by adding element qualifiers. The Dublin Core element convention used in the generic stylesheet is modified to match the digital repository's requirement for batch loading. Edits are made to account for local variance in the application of the MARC format and to account for differences between how the physical item was described versus how the digital item should be described. Fields in MARC that do not belong in the digital record are removed as elements from the stylesheet. Data that applies to every item in the digital collection and is not present in the MARC data is added to the stylesheet to be output for each record.

Step Five: The XSLT stylesheet is processed. The newly modified stylesheet is added to the XSLT folder used by MarcEdit, and the stylesheet is added as an option to the software's XML Conversions function. The new stylesheet is selected and the MARCXML file created previously is the input file. An XML file of Qualified Dublin Core records is the result.

Step Six: Evaluate the records output from the XSLT transformation to determine if the stylesheet functions as expected. If necessary, modify the XSLT stylesheet and rerun the transform.

Step Seven: Add the Qualified Dublin Core records and digital files to the repository. How this is done depends upon the repository software that is used. In this scenario the DSpace software is used, and the records and files are batch loaded into the system using the item importer function.

XSLT Use Case Two: End-User Generated and Harvested Metadata

New Web technologies have increased the sources of metadata available to libraries for the description of their resources. Users of resources are increasingly supplying metadata in the form of usage data, reviews, ratings, tags, comments, and descriptions. End-users are also supplying metadata for the items they self-archive in repositories. In addition, there is more metadata for digital resources available to libraries in recent years due to the use of the Open Archives Initiative Protocol for Metadata Harvesting (OAI-PMH).[27] The library environment has seen an ever increasing number of OAI data providers exposing the metadata in their repositories for others to harvest freely.

Objective

The library has a collection of electronic theses and dissertations (ETDs) in its institutional repository. For this scenario the institutional repository uses DSpace software and is an OAI data provider exposing Simple Dublin Core. The authors of the ETDs add their work to the repository by uploading their digital file and filling out a Web form to add Qualified Dublin Core metadata. The library also has MARC records for the ETDs in the library catalog and in OCLC WorldCat. The records are added to the local catalog and to OCLC by performing original MARC cataloging. The library wants to streamline this workflow and eliminate much of the duplicate effort in describing these resources.

Method

Step One: Determine the relationship between the existing metadata used to describe the digital collection and the description that will be necessary for the library catalog. Using an existing Qualified Dublin Core to MARC crosswalk, modify the map to accommodate local variations and desired outcome.

Step Two: Create a customized XSLT stylesheet to convert the Qualified Dublin Core to MARCXML as represented by the mapping previously created. The OAI (Simple) Dublin Core to MARCXML stylesheet included with the MarcEdit software is used as a template. The caveat here is that the repository only exposes Simple, or Unqualified Dublin Core, while the repository metadata was created using Qualified Dublin Core. The stylesheet, however, uses element positioning to reestablish the Qualified Dublin Core context lost when the metadata is exposed for harvesting as Simple Dublin Core. This MarcEdit stylesheet is edited for local variations of element positioning within item records. The stylesheet is also edited to account for local variance in the application of the Qualified Dublin Core and MARC formats. For example, individual repositories often have different data values for elements such as type. They also may differ in the use of certain Dublin Core elements and how they distinguish the use of dc.creator versus dc.contributor.author. Data that would apply to all MARC records and is not present in the Qualified Dublin Core records is added to the stylesheet if appropriate and the newly modified XSLT stylesheet is added to MarcEdit.

Step Three: The Qualified Dublin Core ETD records are harvested from the library's institutional repository as Simple Dublin Core records. For this scenario Marc-Edit's built-in OAI harvester is used and our new XSLT stylesheet is selected for the transformation. MarcEdit's harvester automates the entire process of harvesting, converting from Simple Dublin Core to MARCXML, and then to MARC all with one click. In other words, MarcEdit's harvester allows for direct Dublin Core to MARC transformations. MarcEdit's harvester also includes the ability, during the same process, to automatically remap metadata from Unicode, the repository encoding, to MARC-8, the library catalog encoding.

Step Four: Evaluate the records output from the XSLT transformation to determine if the stylesheet functions as expected. If necessary, modify the XSLT stylesheet and rerun the transform. Examine the MARC output. MarcEdit's editing functions can be used to clean up the MARC metadata and add or edit fields as needed.

Step Five: Add the MARC records to the library catalog and OCLC. Using Marc-Edit the MARC records can be directly uploaded to OCLC's Connexion cataloging software to make edits if necessary. The Connexion software can also be used to add the original records and holdings to OCLC and to download the records into the local catalog.

The two use cases I have enumerated are but a glimpse of how repurposing metadata with XSLT can be helpful in today's library environment. Successfully repurposing metadata is not without its issues however. In the next section I will briefly present some of the challenges of repurposing metadata.

METADATA REPURPOSING CHALLENGES

One of the first steps of any repurposing project is metadata analysis. Properly analyzing source metadata in relation to the target metadata is vital to reusing data in new environments. There are many things to consider when making metadata transformation decisions. First and foremost is that metadata was created for a specific purpose and for a specific environment. Taking metadata out of its original context can negatively impact the interpretation of that data. For example, metadata created for a local collection may not contain data that pertains to the whole collection if it relied on the local system and/or local collection for that context. When repurposing metadata it is often necessary to augment the metadata by adding contextual information to increase the understandability of the resource when viewed in larger aggregations or via third-party discovery platforms. On the other hand, it is often a good idea to not include all the metadata available when repurposing for a different context. For example, local metadata may contain technical and preservation metadata pertaining to how a digital object was scanned and by whom. This information is very helpful for local administrative and preservation needs but may decrease the usefulness of the metadata when shared beyond local boundaries for resource discovery.

Metadata mapping is never perfect. Metadata schemas vary in granularity, and metadata elements in different schemas rarely match exactly in terms of both semantics and formatting. Data splitting may be necessary where either the data in one field is split into multiple fields or multiple data values in one field are split into repeating fields. The syntax of the data contained in fields also needs to be taken into account. In order to be interpreted correctly when mapped, the data values in the source metadata may need to be transformed, for example, by reversing the order of the author names. Mapping from a hierarchical schema to a flat schema presents particular challenges. Relationships critical to the interpretability of the data can be compromised when flattening a hierarchical schema.

Metadata is often rife with local quirks even when created following community standards and rules. Understanding local metadata creation decisions and policies helps to accurately map metadata and to successfully implement normalizing transformations to prepare the metadata for its new role in the larger community. Metadata standards and practices not only vary with local implementations, but they also vary over time. Legacy metadata that on the surface seems homogenous may have been created using different rules and different interpretations of content standards over the course of its extended creation history.

Metadata quality can vary wildly. Metadata can be inaccurate, incorrect, and incomplete. It can also be inconsistent. Different content standards may have been used across a collection or within individual records. Standards and policies may have been applied differently by individual metadata creators. Metadata can also be insufficient. Metadata may lack documentation of policies and choices made. The content standards used may be difficult to ascertain with just the metadata records themselves. A profile of how schemas and elements were applied during creation may not be available. It is important to not exacerbate this problem when repurposing metadata. The ease of using stylesheets and modifying them on the fly can discourage proper documentation of crosswalks and associated metadata workflows. Decisions made during metadata creation as well as metadata repurposing should be well documented to enhance the reusability of crosswalks outside of a local context.

CONCLUSION

Although there is much to take into account when repurposing metadata it will continue to be an integral component in the metadata management undertaken by libraries. Libraries have invested considerable monetary, intellectual, and temporal resources in their metadata. Repurposing library metadata is also an investment, but it is often a reasonable alternative to duplicative effort in an environment focused on streamlining. Libraries with the desire to provide a Web presence for their resources and simultaneous, seamless access to those resources are taking advantage of the wealth of metadata they possess and converting their legacy data to formats better suited to Web technologies. XSLT is but one way to convert metadata for new purposes, but it is a method that can be quickly adopted by librarians.

NOTES

1. For an introduction to metadata and metadata issues in today's digital environment see Foulonneau, M. and J. Riley. *Metadata for Digital Resources: Implementation, Systems Design and Interoperability.* Oxford: Chandos, 2008; Baca, Murtha, ed., *Introduction to Metadata,* 2nd ed. Version 3.0, Los Angeles: Getty, 2008.

2. Extensible Markup Language (XML) 1.0 (Fifth Edition): W3C Recommendation November 26, 2008. http://www.w3.org/TR/xml/.

3. Lorcan Dempsey has defined interoperability as "the 'recombinant ability' an object has, the ease with which it can be remixed in different combinations to create value." Dempsey, L. "Recombinance All the Way Up ... Remixing All the Way Down." Lorcan Dempsey's Weblog May 6, 2005. http://orweblog.oclc.org/archives/000657.html.

4. XSL Transformations (XSLT) Version 1.0: W3C Recommendation, November 16, 1999. http://www.w3.org/TR/xslt; XSL Transformations (XSLT) Version 2.0: W3C Recommendation, January 23, 2007. http://www.w3.org/TR/xslt20/.

5. The Extensible Stylesheet Language Family (XSL). http://www.w3.org/Style/XSL/.

6. XML Path Language (XPath) Version 1.0: W3C Recommendation, November 16, 1999. http://www.w3.org/TR/xpath; XML Path Language (XPath) 2.0: W3C Recommendation, January23, 2007. http://www.w3.org/TR/xpath20/.

7. Extensible Stylesheet Language (XSL) Version 1.1: W3C Recommendation 05 December 2006. http://www.w3.org/TR/xsl/.

8. Altova XMLSpy. http://www.altova.com/products/xmlspy/xmlspy.html.

9. <oXygen/> XML Editor. http://www.oxygenxml.com/.

10. MSXSL. http://msdn.microsoft.com/xml/.

11. Saxon. http://saxon.sourceforge.net/.

12. Xalan. http://xml.apache.org/xalan-j/index.html.

13. MarcEdit. http://oregonstate.edu/~reeset/marcedit/html/index.php.

14. MADS Style Sheets. http://www.loc.gov/standards/mads/; MARCXML Conversion Style Sheets. http://www.loc.gov/standards/marcxml/; MODS Style Sheets. http://www.loc.gov/standards/mods/mods-conversions.html.

15. ONIX for Books. http://www.editeur.org/onixbooks3.0/onix3.0.html; ONIX for Serials. http://www.editeur.org/onixserials.html.

16. MARCXML. http://www.loc.gov/standards/marcxml/.

17. MARC. http://www.loc.gov/marc/.

18. Innovative Interfaces' Millennium Integrated Library System. http://www.iii.com/products/millennium_ils.shtml.

19. MARCXML Toolkit. http://www.loc.gov/standards/marcxml/.

20. Dublin Core. http://dublincore.org/; Simple and Qualified Dublin Core. http://dublincore.org/schemas/xmls/.

21. MARCXML to OAI Encoded Simple Dublin Core Stylesheet. http://www.loc.gov/standards/marcxml/xslt/MARC21slim2OAIDC.xsl.

22. METS (Metadata Encoding & Transmission Standard). http://www.loc.gov/standards/mets/.

23. MODS (Metadata Object Description Standard). http://www.loc.gov/standards/mods/.

24. PREMIS (Preservation Metadata). http://www.loc.gov/standards/premis/.

25. MIX (NISO Metadata for Images in XML). http://www.loc.gov/standards/mix/.

26. RDA: Resource Description and Access. http://www.rdaonline.org/.

27. Open Archives Initiative Protocol for Metadata Harvesting (OAI-PMH). http://www.openarchives.org/pmh/.

ADDITIONAL READINGS

Dushay, N. and D. I. Hillman. "Analyzing Metadata for Effective Use and Re-use." *International Conference on Dublin Core and Metadata Applications.* Seattle, WA: Dublin Core, 2003. http://dcpapers.dublincore.org/ojs/pubs/article/view/744/740.

Foulonneau, M. and T. W. Cole. "Strategies for Reprocessing Aggregated Metadata." In *Proceedings Series: Lecture Notes in Computer Science.* Heidelberg: Springer-Verlag, 2005. pp. 290–301.

Hillmann, D. I. "Metadata Quality: From Evaluation to Augmentation." *Cataloging & Classification Quarterly* 46, no. 1 (May 2008): 65–80.

Hillmann, D. I., N. Dushay, and J. Phipps. "Improving Metadata Quality: Augmentation and Recombination." *International Conference on Dublin Core and Metadata Applications.* Shanghai, China: DublinCore, 2004. http://dcpapers.dublincore.org/ojs/pubs/article/view/770/766.

Keith, Corey. "Using XSLT to Manipulate MARC Metadata." *Library Hi Tech* 22, no. 2 (2004): 122–30.

Kurth, Martin, David Ruddy, and Nathan Rupp. "Repurposing MARC Metadata: Using Digital Project Experience to Develop a Metadata Management Design." *Library Hi Tech* 22, no. 2 (2004): 153–65.

Lagoze, Carl, Dean Krafft, Tim Cornwell, Naomi Dushay, Dean Eckstrom, and John Saylor. "Metadata Aggregation and 'Automated Digital Libraries': A Retrospective on the NSDL." In *Proceedings of the 6th ACS/IEEE-CS Joint Conference on Digital Libraries* (Chapel Hill, NC, USA, June 11–15, 2006). New York: ACM Press, 2006. pp. 230–39.

St. Pierre, M. and W. P. LaPlant. "Issues in Crosswalking Content Metadata Standards." *NISO.* October 15, 1998. http://www.niso.org/publications/white_papers/crosswalk/.

Reese, Terry. "Automated Metadata Harvesting: Low-Barrier MARC Record Generation from OAI-PMH Repository Stores using MarcEdit." *Library Resources & Technical Services* 53, no. 2 (April, 2009): 121–34.

Reese, Terry. "Bibliographic Freedom and the Future Direction of Map Cataloging." *Journal of Map & Geography Libraries* 2, no. 1 (2005): 67–97.

11

COMMUNICATING
EFFECTIVELY WITH IT

Elizabeth L. Black

Information Technology departments and professionals tend to have a bad reputation with librarians. Eavesdrop at any library conference or gathering of librarians and one will hear complaints about the unresponsive IT department, or worse, the IT group that blocks all progress and stymies attempts to try new things. There are usually one or two librarians who can point to the exception—the IT person who does cool, innovative things and helps them serve patrons in new and creative ways. Most however will sigh and say it is a shame that IT people are so difficult. Why, when both occupations work so hard to provide information and access to their clients, is it so difficult for them to get along? This chapter will explore the similarities and differences between librarians and IT professionals in order to enable better understanding. It will explore models of communication and their implications for work between librarians and IT professionals, and describe strategies librarians can use to build good working relationships with their IT departments. Much of the work between IT and librarians is project based, so this chapter will present techniques to improve project work and effective team building and will conclude with suggestions about formal agreements to help sustain good working relationships.

The traditional rift between librarians and IT departments was recently a topic for the *Chronicle of Higher Education* podcast *Tech Therapy*. Hosts Scott Carlson and Warren Arbogast (2008) explored the similarities and differences of the two groups to gain a better understanding of the culture clash. They noted several differences including the female-dominated library profession and the male-dominated IT profession and the long tradition of library work, which is very value driven, and the relatively new profession of IT, which tends to be more task driven. Another key difference in higher education is the faculty orientation of librarians, many of whom are members of the faculty and, even if they aren't, still have teaching and research responsibilities; the IT departments on the other hand are administrative and professional staff whose work is more directed by their managers and administrators. Carlson and Arborgast pointed out that there are also many similarities between the two groups: both are dealing with rapidly changing work environments, and both groups have an expert attitude that makes them think they know what is best for their users. They concluded their podcast with the message that IT departments and libraries must learn to work together because the future holds more, not fewer, occasions for shared work since both groups are passionate about information, and cost-saving efforts throughout higher education can force "shotgun marriages by executive decree."

TRADITIONAL STEREOTYPES

All stereotypes have a grain of truth in them. For the purpose of encouraging empathy and understanding of IT professionals and librarians, this section will describe the common traits of each group as depicted in stereotypes and recent literature. They are not intended to depict any individuals.

Librarians

Stereotypes of librarians generally include the description of women who are prim and proper, strict, orderly, and old-fashioned. More positive stereotypes describe librarians as introverted yet eager to help those who ask them, organized, smart in an academic or book sense, and experts at finding information. These professionals are likeable individuals who are dedicated to their profession and doing "good" for reasons other than money. Other traits commonly used to describe librarians are detail-oriented and concerned about maintaining order.

Librarians tend to be introverted. Studies of librarian personality types using the Myers-Briggs Type Indicator, a commonly used psychometric instrument, found three common types, specifically ISFJ, INTJ, and ISTJ. All three of these share the trait of introversion (Low 2007).

> ISFJs are *I*ntroverted, *S*ensing, *F*eeling and *J*udging personalities. These individuals prefer to obtain data from their five senses. They like closure. They're often described as responsible and conscientious individuals.
> INTJs are *I*ntroverted, *I*ntuitive, *T*hinking, and *J*udging personalities. They like connections and complexity between things. They're often described as having original minds, being organized, independent, and critical.
> ISTJs are *I*ntroverted, *S*ensing, *T*hinking, and *J*udging personalities. They're often described as orderly, responsible, serious, and practical. (Low 2007, 16)

Many articles and books have been written describing the changes needed in librarians to make them ready for the changes facing the profession. The traits featured in these often include flexibility, curiosity, and being good with technology. The core services often remain the same, such as user assistance and education for reference librarians, and collection development and management for subject librarians (Goetsch 2008). The methods of achieving these aims and the environment within which they occur, however, require different traits and approaches. Goetsch envisions four new core responsibilities: consulting services, information life cycle management, collaborative print and electronic collection building, and information mediation and interpretation.

IT Professionals

Paul Glen, in *Leading Geeks*, describes this group as "the knowledge workers who specialize in the creation, maintenance or support of high technology" (Glen 2003, 4). It is IT professionals who enable innovation involving technology. Glen goes on to state unequivocally, "Geeks are different from other people" (Glen 2003, 11). The key to working well with this group is to understand how they are different and value those differences for the strengths they bring.

Traits noted by Glen include a passion for reason, a problem-solution mind-set, joy of puzzles, curiosity, preference for machines, belief that self-expression is the same as communication, a confusion of facts and opinions, swift judgment, viewing work as art, reverence for geek smarts, loyalty to technology and profession, belief in meritocracy, and great value for independence.

The passion for reason means that all decisions must be based on solid logic. Reason and logic pair nicely with the problem-solving mind-set. It takes a logical mind to identify the problem in a system and then to find a solution. The danger in these traits is being too quick to settle on *the* problem to be solved. Gerald Weinberg (1986) describes a state known as "no-problem syndrome" when a programmer responds "No problem!" to the description of an issue in full confidence that he can provide a solution but then cannot adequately describe the issue facing the client.

Self-expression, that is, stating ones position or point of view, is not the same as communication, which will be described in more detail later. However, many technical people have this misconception. They will state their point and move on to other tasks never checking for understanding and clarity. This, combined with the trait to state as fact and with passion opinions about the validity of specific technical products or configurations, can exacerbate communication challenges.

Technical work is ultimately a creative process. Rightfully so, the creators take great pride in their creations. Those who critique them should do so carefully. On a related note, those who expect a programmer to precisely estimate the time needed to write the code is setting the stage for disappointment. That is the same as asking an artist to predict the time it takes to complete a masterpiece before it is even begun.

Within the geek subculture, technical knowledge is held in high regard. Those who demonstrate and share their technical knowledge effectively become leaders in the field. Technical people, similar to many academics, are loyal first to their profession. They may change jobs but often remain in the same technical area of expertise.

A recent *Computerworld* article (Eckle 2008) reported the Myers-Briggs Type Indicator types for common roles in IT. Software developers are generally INTP (*I*ntrovert, *I*ntuitive, *T*hinking, and *P*erceiving); they have an abstract view of the world and enjoy continuously learning new skills and trying new techniques to build complex solutions. They like to keep things open and might show little interest in implementation. Types such as ENTJ (*E*xtrovert, *I*ntuitive, *T*hinking, *J*udging) or INTJ (*I*ntrovert, *I*ntuitive, *T*hinking, *J*udging) become the leaders of programming groups because their J helps them to serve as a bridge with the more concrete outside world. Those who are drawn to tech support are typically ESFP (*E*xtrovert, *S*ensing, *F*eeling, *P*erceiving) or ESTP (*E*xtrovert, *S*ensing, *T*hinking, *P*erceiving) because they are good troubleshooters and work well with people.

FOCUS ON STRENGTHS

The descriptions of each group above included items that can be interpreted in both a negative and positive manner. Identifying the positive aspects of traits and working toward enhancing the strengths they represent will go a long way toward building positive working relationships between librarians and technology professionals.

The traits that make librarians good librarians are some of the same ones that aid working on technical projects and working with technical professionals. Curiosity and perseverance, traits of great reference and cataloging librarians, readily applied to interactions with IT professionals make communication go more smoothly. Ask those questions. Do a modified reference interview to make sure needs are heard and understood. Show interest in the expertise of the technical colleague and a willingness to learn the language.

Librarians, especially those in small libraries, demonstrate flexibility daily. They switch quickly from task to task and role to role as they teach classes, supervise student workers and paraprofessional staff, and do their own research. This flexibility applied to working in technical projects means taking on different roles in the project and adapting to the issues and challenges that appear.

The natural curiosity of most librarians is a great asset. Learn about the technology and show a genuine interest in the area of expertise of the IT professionals.

Librarians traditionally have relied on collaborations and cooperative work to accomplish daunting tasks; look to OCLC and other library consortia for evidence of this trait. Attention to detail and desire for order combined with this collaborative spirit have led to solid organizations that have withstood the test of time.

Likewise the traits that stereotypically describe IT professionals can be important assets. The tasks and projects librarians generally bring to their IT colleagues are often classified as problems, and so a person with a problem-solving dispensation who values reason and technical smarts is an asset to the situation. This person generally derives satisfaction from finding the solution, so describing issues as problems or even as puzzles to be solved might ignite the natural desire to seek resolution.

Creativity combined with technical knowledge leads to successful innovations. Honoring the sense of ownership that comes with the creativity will go far in working with technical experts. Being honest about the difficulty of setting timelines in these situations will facilitate understanding and respect.

Both occupations tend to be more introverted and more thinking on the Myers-Briggs Type Indicator scales. These are areas of common approaches upon which to build understanding. All of the librarian types contained J, which tends to prefer things to be finished, while several of the IT types, significantly programmers, contained P, which tends to prefer things left open-ended. This is an area of potential conflict but ultimately balances the project teams that contain both traits.

COMMUNICATION

Communication involves much more than simply the words said. The nonverbal portion of in-person communication conveys more of the message than the verbal portion. A significant aspect of communication is the interpretation of all of this information by the person receiving the message. Human beings are complex and many factors go into the interpretation of a message.

Where a person is on Maslow's (1954) hierarchy of needs can have a big impact on how that person interprets a message. Those whose current needs are on the lower part of the hierarchy, physiological and safety needs, are very motivated by external factors such as wages, job security, and similar external motivators. Most of the people involved in libraries and IT generally have these needs met. That moves individuals to the next three levels, which Maslow identified as the higher-order needs: social, self-esteem, and self-actualization. At the social level, a person seeks acceptance and a sense of belonging. The important thing to note in communicating with individuals at this level is the group to which this person seeks to belong. In *Leading Geeks* Paul Glen (2003) notes that geek culture is often a subculture within organizations that value nonconformity.

The self-esteem level on the hierarchy seeks to meet the needs of self-respect as well as status and recognition from others. The value of the peer group noted at the third level has bearing here as well; Glen notes that geeks earn status through displays of knowledge and technical prowess.

The final level, self-actualization, involves the need for self-fulfillment, to grow and achieve one's full potential. This state might be likened to the level-five leader described by Jim Collins (2008), a person who is both modest and willful. These unusual people possess strength of character, including a solid understanding of their personal strengths and weaknesses, as well as a compelling vision and unwavering resolve to achieve their full potential.

Persons operating at the final level of Maslow's hierarchy are rare, and even then individuals can move between levels based on circumstances. Understanding that individuals interpret messages based on many different factors, much more than the words themselves, aids those in the communication to identify issues more quickly and modify approaches to diffuse potentially difficult situations. Gerald Weinberg (1986) used Virginia Satir's work in this area to flesh out a model of interactions; his focus was preparing technical professionals for leadership roles. The model of interaction has seven steps: (1) sensory input, (2) interpretation, (3) feeling, (4) feeling about the feeling, (5) defense, (6) rules for commenting, and (7) outcome.

The sensory input includes the words as well as the tone of voice, body language, and other nonverbal cues. This input is not perfect; the sender assumes that the message was clear, but it is best to expect that something will be lost in every reception. At this step, those seeking to improve should work on improving the accuracy of their own reception abilities and watching for signs when sending messages that the receiver may have lost part of the input.

The interpretation step takes place on the message actually received (not necessarily the one sent), and it is based on the receiver's past experience. This could be a recent or long-past experience; it could be with the same individuals or with others in the receiver's past. Understanding this step makes communicators aware that several interpretations are possible and that they cannot anticipate all of them.

At the third step, the feeling step, the receiver reacts with a feeling about the interpretation made of the message. Once the interpretation is made, the feeling just happens. This all happens very quickly; at this point in the model only seconds have elapsed. The important point at this step for a receiver working to improve communication skills is to become aware of the feeling related to the interpretation and to differentiate it from other emotions.

In the fourth step of the interaction model, the receiver now reacts to the feeling in step three with another feeling. Weinberg points out that this critical point is based on the receiver's feeling of self-worth and is most likely associated with a survival rule this person learned early in life. If the receiver is feeling good about herself, she is more likely to accept the feeling but not react only to the feeling. If the receiver is feeling poorly about herself, she is more likely to feel negative feelings more strongly and follow a survival rule blindly. Becoming aware of one's own survival rules and common feelings about feelings in communication situations helps communicators be open to the real and intended messages instead of blindly following survival rules. It also helps senders to be more objective when others react unexpectedly to messages.

The defense step affects those with poor self-worth the most. Those who feel that they should not be feeling as they do about the message (say the receiver feels afraid and in step four feels ashamed of being afraid) will mount a defense to stop those feelings. If, on the other hand, the receiver has a stronger self-worth, he might accept the feeling and move on to the next stage. Defenses might include projecting the problem onto another person, ignoring the feelings, denying the feelings, or distorting them. In stage six the receiver has produced an internal response. Before making a public response, the receiver considers the internal response in light of any personal or internal rules that might apply to the situation. The actual response, or outcome, occurs in step seven; all six preceding steps occurred in less than a minute. Clues about the preceding internal and nonverbal steps are present in the tone of voice and body language. These clues are important elements to resolving communication interactions that go awry. Weinberg notes five reasons why messages get confused moving through the stages. The first is perception; each person is unique so even the most straightforward of messages will be perceived differently. The second, wrong time, occurs when the transformation of the message through the interaction model refers to things in the past or the future and have no logical bearing on the current situation. Wrong place, the third reason for confusing communication, occurs when the transformation refers to a context other than the current one. Wrong person, the fourth reason, occurs when the message transformation and reaction are in reaction to another person in the receiver's experiences, not the sender of the current message. The fifth reason, feelings of self-worth, has powerful impacts on both parties to the communication. Due to the complexity of the model and the multiple ways in which communication can go awry, "Satir estimates that ninety percent of all communications are incongruent, inconsistent with what we truly want to communicate." (Weinberg 1986, 114–15) Incongruent communication is the source of many difficulties between coworkers.

Paradoxically, the most effective way to resolve communication challenges is to make one's own path through the model transparent to the person with whom one is trying to communicate. Weinberg suggests this formula: "Tell them what you perceive, how you feel about what you perceive, and if possible how you feel about that feeling" (115).

EXAMPLE OF COMMUNICATION MODELS IN ACTION

Mary is an instruction librarian in a small academic library. Her Myers-Briggs Type Indicator is ISTJ. Traits of this type include being task-oriented, logical, and having a need to see things finished. She has been in her position only a year, so she is at the social level on the Maslow scale. Mary is comfortable using web-based tools and wants to use more technology in her library instruction. She has not written any code and has a limited technical vocabulary.

Bob is a programmer/systems manager with the campus web service on which the library Web site is hosted. His Myers-Briggs Type Indicator is INTP. Traits of this type include a dislike of rules, a tendency to improvise, and a preference to leave things open-ended. He is at the social level on the Maslow scale; the group he wants to fit in with, however, is other programmers. He has not worked with Mary before but has had challenging interactions with other librarians in the past.

Mary wants to use a wiki and a blog on the library Web site. She e-mails Bob seeking to find out if he could add this software to the Web site. He does not respond in the timeline she expects, so she e-mails a follow-up message asking for a meeting. He agrees. At the meeting, she explains in what she thinks is a very logical way that she wants to use a blog to share instruction tips and stories about using the library and a wiki for creating resource guides with other librarians. Mary provides great detail about what she will be doing with the blog and wiki, thinking it will help Bob meet the need. He begins to fiddle with his phone and appears to be only half listening. Then he interrupts Mary asking what her requirements are. She is taken aback because she has just been describing them. She tries again, saying that she wants a blog and a wiki for instruction. He now thinks she has no idea what she is talking about and says, "No problem. I can get you those." Mary is relieved and thanks Bob and ends the meeting.

Three weeks later Mary has not heard from Bob and she is getting worried. She has shared with her colleague that she is working on getting a blog and a wiki and they are all excited. She calls Bob on the phone to ask about the status of her request. He replies that they are working on it. She asks if there is anything he needs from her and he says no. The conversation ends there. After three more weeks, she again calls Bob, who still has nothing to share but assures her that they are working on it.

Bob has indeed been exploring blogs and wikis. He is trying to find the one he thinks is the best written and will be the easiest to run on the Web site. He has tried several, tinkering with each to find the one that will be the easiest for the librarians, who in his previous experience are bad with technology. He has shared his explorations with his coworkers, proudly showing the improvements he has made. He has not shared any of this with Mary because of his belief that nontechnical people can't appreciate his work. He doesn't know that Mary is good with web applications and that she has even used a hosted blog at home.

Finally, after several more weeks have passed, Mary schedules a meeting with Bob. She is very frustrated because she thinks that Bob has not kept his word and that no progress is being made on her request. Bob is frustrated because Mary keeps nagging him and suggesting that he has not done anything when he has done all of this work finding the best tools. At the meeting, Mary states that she needs a blog and wiki now so she can be ready for the semester that is starting next week. Bob interprets this as a reaffirmation that his work is not appreciated by librarians and he feels angry. He then feels ashamed that he has let a nontechnical person insult his work and gets defensive. He responds angrily that this was not in the original request, that he is working on it, and she will get it when he is done. Both leave the meeting more frustrated than ever.

How could this have gone better? Let's return to the initial meeting. If at that meeting either Mary or Bob had taken more time to clarify the request and the expectations, much of this difficulty would have been avoided. If Mary had done a little bit of research first to know what type of platform the Web site was on and a few of the common blogs and wikis used on this type of platform, she may have grabbed Bob's attention with her attempt to understand the technology. She should also have stated the deadlines clearly and negotiated check-in meetings to review progress. If Bob had noted that Mary didn't understand his initial requirements question and asked it in a different way, he would have been able to narrow down his exploration. Mary might ask Bob a few questions to figure out what he meant by his requirements question when she realized that they were not communicating. He should also have noted when the items were needed and in what order. If he did not, Mary might offer this information. He could have asked about Mary's use of these tools to get an idea of her technical level.

At the follow-up conversations, Bob could have shared what he had done so far. Mary would then have seen that he was doing something on her request. In these situations, it would be important for Mary to note the things that she liked first and then make suggestions about what might be done differently, being sure at all times to show that she respected Bob's work. Once Mary saw which tool Bob was using, it would serve her well to learn more about it on her own so she could knowledgeably discuss the tool.

Due to his INTP type, Bob is inclined to improvise and explore options without urgency to decide. Mary, with her ISTJ type, wants to see order and steady progress toward completion of the project. There is bound to be conflict with these different approaches, so it is important that each of them note their feelings. Mary might say that she is feeling anxious about meeting the deadline and that it will help her to know what the remaining tasks are so she has a better understanding. This is much less likely to cause Bob to feel defensive and angry than just asking how long it will take.

PROJECT WORK

The work of many librarians is ongoing; things like staffing the reference desk, bibliographic instruction, and cataloging materials are regular occurrences. This operational work differs significantly from project work, which for the purposes of the ARL Project Management Institute (2007) is defined as "a series of non-routine tasks directed toward a goal." Much of IT work is project-based and follows a project life cycle. Each stage of the project builds on the work in the previous stage. In the simplest terms, a project has a beginning, middle, and an end; different tasks are critical in each stage. Disciplined planning and clear roles for members of the project team are key parts of the process involved in bringing successful projects to completion. The focus on process and documentation, especially in the beginning phases of a project, often strikes librarians and programmers alike as needless process and bureaucracy. Particularly when the idea for the project starts with the librarian, the project definition and team recruitment stages can seem especially long-winded. But it is here where the key goals are outlined, the scope determined, and the resources acquired. Moving too quickly to "doing" without planning often leads to significant conflicts later. Tinkering and exploring can be effective parts of the definition and planning stage but must not be mistaken for implementation.

The stages of a project are concept, definition, planning, execution, and closeout (Lewis 2006). Notice that the first three stages take place before any of the real work on the final project gets done. But these first three stages are critical to the outcome of the project because it is during these stages that the group comes to a shared understanding about what the problem is they are trying to solve and the means by which it will be solved. The products of these stages document the decisions made. Without doing this, the project becomes a "headless-chicken project" that has lots of activity but no direction and low chance of a positive outcome (Lewis 2006).

In the concept and definition stages the goals of the project are spelled out, the desired outcomes described, and the members of the project team assembled. In the concept stage the idea is conceived and initial support from the organizational leadership is obtained in order to create a project team. During the definition stage, each member of the project and the administration agree on the scope of the project: what is to be accomplished and what is not to be accomplished. This might take the form of a project vision and mission statement or a project charter. For programming projects, a requirements-gathering process occurs. This critical step in the definition stage takes the goals and fleshes out the details. In a corporate environment, this process is often performed by a business analyst. Many libraries do not have a person dedicated to this role in the organization so will need to find someone else to perform it. Gathering the requirements for the software to be developed or for the technology outcome needed to meet the goal might be thought of as an extended reference interview. The use of open, closed, and neutral questions in varying ways uncovers the requirements of the technical need just as they do an information need. The business analyst asks many questions and in the best case observes the problem or need the project is meant to solve. This person then writes up a document noting the specifications for the end product. In an agile project management environment, this might be done in a group using a paper prototyping technique. No matter how it is done, the key is to produce detailed documentation noting the goals and specific outcomes expected from the project.

In the planning stage, the project team outlines the strategy for achieving the goals and identifies the tasks required. The questions to be answered during the planning stage are (Lewis 2006):

- What must be done?
- How should it be done?
- Who will do it?
- By when must it be done?
- How much will it cost?
- How good does it have to be?

The answers to these questions are documented in the project plan, which is usually maintained by the project manager. The project manager documents the tasks, with input from the other members of the team, breaking them into milestones or phases. Project managers must also track the time it will take to perform each task, dependencies among tasks, and other factors that will impact the project, such as other projects happening simultaneously or ongoing maintenance or operational work.

Project managers, another common full-time position in a corporate environment, are rare in libraries. It is, however, an essential role for projects and can be filled by a librarian or another member of the library staff. This role requires strong organizational and communication skills. Lewis cautions against having a project team member serve both as project manager and another role in the group because that person will inevitably feel torn between doing the tasks associated with each role and generally will neglect the management tasks.

The quality of the project plan is tested during the execution stage. It is at this stage that the work on the project's product is performed. The project manager monitors progress using the project plan. Team members perform the tasks assigned; regular project meetings ensure coordination between members and tracking of progress by the project manager. Inevitably unexpected problems will arise or circumstances will change but if the project definition and plan are strong and all team members have a shared understanding of the goal, corrective action occurs more smoothly.

The final project stage, closeout, is a review of the project. In many organizations, unfortunately, this gets skipped. In all of the excitement over releasing the product of the project, the team may be reluctant to review the project itself for fear that it will take away from the success. The opposite is true. The closeout phase identifies the methods that proved successful in the current project so they can be applied to future projects. Lessons for improvements are also identified but not in the context of what went wrong; instead, the focus is on lessons and improvements that might be applied to future projects. This stage also provides the opportunity for closure for the team members, which makes the adjourning phase described later easier.

TEAM WORK

Most project work is done in teams. Often these teams are formed for the duration of the project only. Effective work teams don't just happen; they are formed. Teams differ from working groups because they require both individual and shared accountability; they require discipline. According to Jon Katzenbach and Douglas Smith (1993, 112), "a team is a small number of people with complementary skills who are committed to a common purpose, set of performance goals, and approach for which they hold themselves mutually accountable."

A common purpose is critical to team formation. This purpose ideally comes during the definition stage of the project. At this stage the forming team sets the ground rules for their performance and decides on the means of accountability. This can be either formal or informal; however, the more open this forming process is the clearer the shared understandings will be.

Bruce Tuckman (2001) created a widely cited model for team development. He noted that teams go through five stages: forming, storming, norming, performing, and adjourning. During the forming stage the members introduce themselves and embark on tentative and polite interactions. At this stage the leader has an active role in communicating purpose and setting expectations to orient the members to the task. The storming stage is one of conflict as team members begin to negotiate roles and make decisions; there is intragroup conflict as members have an emotional response to the task demands. Leadership is critical at this stage to provide support and coaching as the members learn to communicate honestly and respectfully to resolve the conflicts and come to a shared purpose. Next is the norming phase during which in-group feeling and cohesiveness develop, new standards evolve, new roles are adopted, and open exchange of information and opinions is effective because the group members are open to one another. At the performing stage, the team exhibits high performance toward their goals; roles become flexible and functional; conflicts and structural issues are resolved quickly as group energy is channeled into the task; and solutions emerge. The adjourning stage, which Tuckman added later, based on subsequent studies, is a stage of closure and self-evaluation. This stage is marked by both celebration of the completion of the task and sadness and anxiety about separation and termination.

Successful teams have complementary skills among their members, and each member does equivalent amounts of real work that contribute in concrete ways to the team's goal. Therefore, good team leaders select members on the basis of their skills or potential to develop the needed skills. During the establishment of the team, the leader sets the tone for the project. In librarian/IT projects, the leader often is the librarian with the idea for the project, so this person should set a positive tone and establish a compelling need for the project to engage the members. Early on it is also important to set standards for team-member expectations, such as all team members will get assignments and complete them on time. Katzenbach and Smith (1993) note that in successful teams each member of the team does equivalent amounts of work and that the team members hold each other accountable. Successful teams spend lots of time together and the leader makes opportunities for this to happen, especially in the forming and storming phases. Finally, positive feedback, recognition, and reward are powerful motivators to teams and the individual members. A good team leader watches for opportunities to recognize good contributions and finds ways to celebrate successes as a team.

FORMAL AGREEMENTS

Formal, written agreements are regular occurrences with vendors and outsourced services, such as digitizing of fragile books, cleaning services, and so forth. These documents outline the responsibilities of each party and the conditions for the agreement and can be very useful when working with IT groups as well. Formal agreements take several forms; they might be at the level of written documentation to support a project, such as a project charter, or formal Memorandums of Understanding (MOU) or Service Level Agreements (SLA), which have legal standing.

Written documents outlining the shared understanding of all parties to the agreement are opportunities to clarify expectations and to draw out assumptions that can derail work later. For project-based agreements, the documents should outline the goals and objectives of the project, the scope of the project, what items are not part of this project, and the rough time expectation for the project's completion. The project documents should also note the roles of each group in the project at various stages of the project, such as when it is appropriate to add new features and when work is to be approved and by whom. The documents described in this section are about outlining the behavior and expectations of the parties to the agreement, not the requirements of the project's product itself. Often in the excitement of project initiation these documents are not created, causing challenges later.

Once the projects are completed or the equipment installed, there will be an ongoing business relationship to support the product of the shared efforts. Clear and precise communication is once again important. Expectations of each group, including level of support and response time must be negotiated. The roles and expectations of each group, such as timely alerting about changes in personnel and the protocol for dealing with urgent problems, are outlined. Due to the ongoing nature of these relationships, especially if they cross organizational boundaries, these documents often take the form of MOU or SLA. As these are formal agreements with legal understanding, they are often signed by the director of the library and that person's counterpart in the IT organization.

CONCLUSION

Librarians and Information Technology professionals have much in common. Both are experts in some aspect of the information field and are adapting to rapidly changing work environments. Both professions value creativity and expertise. Building on these similarities and sharing a respect for their differences can become the basis of successful working relationships between IT professionals and librarians. Paying attention to the complexities of communication interactions and the significance of unspoken needs and interpretations will resolve and eliminate incongruent communication and other communication challenges. These efforts will facilitate the building of strong project teams that benefit both IT and libraries.

REFERENCES

Association of Research Libraries. Project Management Institute. Workshop held at OSU Libraries, Columbus, OH, May 2–3, 2007. http://library.osu.edu/sites/staff/arlpm/ (accessed March 9, 2009).

Carlson, Scott and Warren Arbogast. "Libraries vs. IT Departments." *Chronicle of Higher Education Audio: Tech Therapy,* no. 33, October 9, 2008, audio: http://chronicle.com/media/audio/v55/i07/techtherapy/ (accessed 3/9/2009), transcript: http://www.bouldermanagementgroup.com/pages/tt/TTLibraries VsITDepartments.pdf (accessed 3/31/2009).

Collins, Jim. "Level 5 Leadership: The Triumph of Humility and Fierce Resolve." In *Business Leadership: A Jossey-Bass Reader,* 2nd edition, edited by Joan V. Gallos, 99–114. San Francisco: John Wiley & Sons, 2008.

Eckle, Jamie. Do You Know Your Type? *Computerworld* 42, no. 35 (2008): 44.

Glen, Paul. *Leading Geeks: How to Manage and Lead People Who Deliver Technology.* San Francisco: Jossey-Bass, 2003.

Goetsch, Lori. "Reinventing Our Work: New and Emerging Roles for Academic Librarians." *Journal of Library Administration* 48, no. 2 (2008): 157–72.

Katzenbach, Jon, and Douglas Smith. "The Discipline of Teams. *Harvard Business Review* 71, no. 2 (1993): 111–20.

Lewis, James P. *Fundamentals of Project Management,* 3rd edition. n.p.: Amacom, 2006. http://proquest.safaribooksonline.com/9780814408797 (accessed March 10, 2009).

Low, Kathleen. *Casanova Was a Librarian: A Light-Hearted Look at the Profession.* Jefferson, NC: McFarland & Company, 2007.

Maslow, Abraham H. *Motivation and Personality.* New York: Harper and Row, 1954.

Tuckman, Bruce W. "Developmental Sequence in Small Groups." *Group Facilitation: A Research and Applications Journal* 3 (2001): 66–81. (reprint of article in *Psychological Bulletin* 63, no. 6 (1965): 384–99.)

Weinberg, Gerald M. *Becoming a Technical Leader: An Organic Problem-Solving Approach.* New York: Dorset House, 1986.

GLOSSARY

Hector Escobar

Access Control a verified process that limits access to resources on a computing system. Access can be controlled by stored tables that verify rights to resources and programs to users who have proper authorization.

aDORe a digital storage system developed by Los Alamos National Laboratory. It works on a write-once/read-many times principle. The process works by combining two different, but interconnected file-based storage mechanisms.

API see Application Programming Interface

Application Programming Interface an interface that is established by a set of functions or rules and allows programs to access and share information within a particular application.

Attribute Assertion a system or process in which characters or data are verified, such as when a valid password is recognized from an invalid one.

Authentication a process that attempts to identify a user and checks for verification of identity.

Authorization a process that verifies allowed access to data.

Bit Rot sometimes referred to as data decay, this is the gradual decay of media storage devices containing data. When this decay takes place, it ultimately affects data that is stored on these devices.

Blackboard a term associated with products from Blackboard Inc. This includes a series of educational course management systems.

Blog a journal that is either personal or belongs to members of a certain group and is posted online. The intent of the blog is to share thoughts, interests, dislikes, reflections, and quick tips of information to online communities based by interest. Bloggers are those who author or update blogs on a regular basis.

Born Digital a phrase used to define objects that are originally created in digital form.

CAS see Central Authentication Service

Cascading Style Sheet a layout style of establishing HTML or XML text within a browser. It was designed with emphasis to separate document content from document layout such as colors, fonts, and so forth. Standards on this style sheet are maintained by the World Wide Web Consortium.

Central Authentication Service designed to allow a user to access multiple software applications or resources by a single log-in. It also allows other applications that require authentication access without retrieving security credentials each time the application is accessed.

Chronopolis a digital preservation project headed by the Library of Congress. Preservation takes place among partner institutions, which store and manage data. The data is then replicated like that of LOCKSS.

Cloud Computing a visual form of computing that allows individuals to use and access services via the Internet. These clouds, or environments, utilize services that are unique to a particular domain but do not necessary require expertise to use.

CMS see Content Management Systems, see Course Management Systems

Coalition of Networked Information composed of over 200 institutions, this organization's goals are to develop and manage networked information content and to build and promote technological standards.

Communicating with IT spoken or written communication that contains and supports terminology that is unique to information technology environments. An example would be calling the help desk and explaining a technical problem over the phone.

Content Management Systems software that allows for managing of content on a Web site. Content managers have the ability to create and edit Web site and database content, usually in a collaborative manner with other departments within an organization.

Course Level Support content that is developed exclusively for a particular course within a learning management system. In some instances it involves the teacher working with a librarian to ensure a library presence within the online course.

Course Management Systems a term that is often referred to as a Learning Management System. System software allows for the delivery of course content and other functions, such as posting syllabi and recording of grades. Some examples of course management systems include WebCT and Blackboard.

CSS see Cascading Style Sheet

Cultural Heritage Data data that is centered on culture and arts within the humanities. It ranges from pictures to oral histories to digital artifacts.

Cyclical Redundancy Check one of the widely used methods for detecting errors in which added digits are calculated from the receiving end to ensure accuracy from the original source.

DAITSS see Dark Archive in the Sunshine State

Dark Archive a closed or public inaccessible digital archive. Its purpose is to act as a backup or repository for information in the event of a disaster.

Dark Archive in the Sunshine State an example of a digital preservation repository system. It was created by the Florida Center for Library Automation with an intention of being the back end to other systems. It is considered a "dark archive" since there is no public interface or public access.

Data Curation management and cycling of data that includes its starting point, promotion, possible sharing and reusing of data, and finally the preservation of data.

Data Deluge a term given to the overabundance of data that is generated by research and computing.

Data Visualization data that is displayed visually in an established flow or schematic form to indicate process, impact, and involvement of data.

Digital Data data that is comprised of information in its basic form of bits that can be interpreted by a computer and computing process.

Digital Library Federation an association of international libraries whose goal is to incorporate technical standards and promote best practices, and which serves as a guide for the creation and preservation of scholarly and cultural digital data.

Digital Preservation System a system that is designed for the preservation of data over extended periods of time. The system should allow for storage, migration, and future reformatting of data.

Digital Repository an online repository that allows individuals to store and access digital objects such as papers, theses, dissertations, and other archival material. Content that is gathered or placed into a digital repository is usually unique to the organization or institution.

Digital Rights Management a term that is given to systems that check for access or authorization of data based on ownership or property rights. An example of a DRM system is Apple and its use within the iTunes Store.

Distributed Computing a computing process that allows a program to divide into segments that run or operate on multiple systems over a distributed network.

DRM see Digital Rights Management

Drupal a PHP and open source software, it is designed to operate as a foundation system for a variety of different Web sites. It also functions as a basic content management system.

DSpace an open source software system released in 2002. The system includes a number of digital preservation tools which covers many types of digital data. Items such as photographs, data sets, books, and videos can all be preserved using this system.

Elastic Compute Cloud a form of cloud computing, it is a service created by Amazon that provides individuals the opportunity to rent computers in order to run programs or process computing.

Electronic Frontier Foundation founded in 1990, this nonprofit organization emphasizes defending the public's rights as it relates to digital content.

Embedded Librarian a term given to a style of librarianship in which a librarian is immersed within a class or environment. This allows the librarian to get a better understanding of research needed by the class or unit and gives individuals greater exposure to the librarian for research assistance.

Emulators a computing program or system that produces the same output from what is received. In other words, a device or system that copies or emulates information or data from an original system.

EPrints an open source software package developed in 2000. The intended use for this system is for institutional digital repositories and online journal publications.

eXtensible Markup Language often referred to as XML, it is a markup language used in tagging documents and data on the Web and allows for enhancements that HTML cannot provide. HTML by itself is used to display content on the Web, but that is its limitation. XML allows for the definition of content contained within text from a Web site. It can be used by itself or with HTML simultaneously.

Extensible Style Language Formatting Objects a markup language that formats XML documents into Adobe's Portable Document Format (PDF).

Extensible Style Language Transformation a programming language that converts documents written in XML into documents of other formats. For example, a page written in XML can be converted by XSLT to be read by a word processing program such as Microsoft Word.

EZproxy a proxy server software program that is used by libraries to control access from outside a library's domain or network. It allows libraries to grant access to individuals trying to access databases or other resources by an authenticating process.

FDA see Florida Digital Archive

Federated Identity Management a federated process of verifying a user. A user has to log in just once to allow access to multiple points or programs and may extend past organizational boundaries for access.

Federated Search the ability to search multiple databases or web resources at the same time by entering just one set of syntax. The search then processes the entered syntax search on multiple resources and produces a unified group listing of results.

Florida Digital Archive serving the state of Florida, this digital archive provides for the preservation of digital material supporting research and scholarship.

F/OSS see Free and Open Source Software

Free and Open Source Software software that is developed with the intention of being shared and distributed widely. The source code is intended to be changed, studied, and improved through this sharing and distribution process. Some popular examples of open source software include Linux and Mozilla.

Free Software Foundation founded in 1985, this foundation is dedicated to distributing free software. Its main emphasis of distribution is with UNIX software.

Freeware software that is free to download or acquire. The software is often a "lite" version of the original. In order to obtain a full version, a user has to purchase a copy of the software, which is then added like a patch to the existing freeware version.

FSF see Free Software Foundation

GNU General Public License a license that allows recipients of computer programs the rights associated with free software for noncommercial applications. It is promoted by the Free Software Foundation.

Google Documents also referred to as Google Docs, this free web-based software suite includes a word processor, spreadsheet, and presentation program. Its web-based feature allows individuals to share and work on certain projects in a collaborative environment, regardless of location.

HTML see Hypertext Markup Language

HTTP see Hypertext Transfer Protocol

Hypertext Markup Language the language for creating basic web pages, it is commonly used on many Web sites. It is a structured language that uses tags for controlling the display of elements such as text, headers, lists, text boxes, images, and so forth.

Hypertext Transfer Protocol an Internet protocol that is a standard for transferring information across the World Wide Web.

Identity Management the life cycle of users' identity information within an organization. This cycle takes into account the many attributes that may exist at various levels for users associated within an organization.

IMS Global Learning Consortium a consortium that began in 1997 from an EDU-CAUSE initiative. Its goal is the development and adoption of technological standards that are based within the learning experience.

Incongruent Communication a communication process in which the sender conveys messages at various levels and the receiver or listener is unable to accept or interpret.

Information Silos software systems that are unable to communicate or transfer information with other systems. This inability creates silos that may be unique in operation but fail to integrate with content from other systems.

Information Visualization data or pieces of information that are represented in a visual model in an attempt to show data in a more significant manner and to give a picture to what may seem abstract as it relates to data.

Institutional Repository a holding space for digital records and objects. Repositories are searchable and allow for preservation and access of material that may have once only existed in nondigital formats.

Integrated Communication Tools communication tools that are included in system software such as a learning management system. These tools allow members to communicate within a certain environment without having to migrate to another Web site or launch a new program.

Integrated Library System a library computer system that allows each module to share information within the system. Some module examples include circulation, serial management, cataloging, and the OPAC. Each module is somewhat dependent on each other in order to process or show detailed information.

Interoperable systems systems that are comprised from other individual systems, that are managed separately, but cooperate collectively in order to produce greater services or operations as a whole.

IP Authentication a process in which an Internet Protocol address is obtained from a location or computer and is identified and granted access depending on access rights.

IR see Institutional Repository

JavaScript Object Notation a markup language that is sometimes used as an alternative to XML; it is a language that allows for data interchanges. It is considered to be lighter and faster than XML.

JSON see JavaScript Object Notation

Kernel the prime and initial software layer within an operating system. This layer has direct initial interaction with system hardware and is responsible for hardware allocations operating within the system software.

LDAP see Lightweight Directory Access Protocol

Learning Management Systems software that is often delivered or accessed via the Web that allows for training and tracking of certain skill sets or competencies.

Legacy Data a term often used to describe information or data that is on an old or obsolete format or computing system.

Lightweight Directory Access Protocol developed in the early 1990s, it serves as a protocol established to query and verify directory information on a network for individuals associated with an organization. This protocol allows administrators to assign rights and define access for users on an LDAP network.

Link Resolver a term classifying software utilities that allow individuals to check online and local print holdings that correspond to citation information found from various library databases.

LMS see Learning Management Systems

LOCKSS see Lots of Copies Keep Stuff Safe

Lots of Copies Keep Stuff Safe this is an open source software system developed at Stanford University. It is a digital preservation software that allows libraries to preserve digital content and provide access at the same time.

Manakin developed at Texas A&M, this user interface provides the ability for an institution to give a look and feel outside of DSpace and into a particular institution's web presence.

MARC 21 developed for the 21st century, MARC 21 is the combined standard MARC record format using both formats from the United States and Canada.

MarcEdit a software editing program developed by Terry Reese, it gives the operator the ability to perform mass batch editing of MARC records.

MARCXML an XML schema developed by the Library of Congress that allows XML to be used with MARC standards.

Mashup often used with APIs, it consists of a web-page application that combines one or more functions into a new function or operation. An example is Google Maps and how Google allows data to be combined with other sources of data, such as real estate data, for locating properties from a realtor's Web site.

MediaWiki a PHP-based wiki licensed under the GNU General Public License, this wiki is an open source software and is the operating software for Wikipedia.

Memorandum of Understanding a formal document which is drafted in agreement with two or more parties. The purpose of this document is to outline rules, principles, and limits within working relationships.

Metadata a term used in describing a grouping or set of data that provides information about other additional data. A database that accesses information from other data sources is an example of metadata usage.

Metadata Encoding and Transmission Standard an XML schema standard used for encoding descriptions for objects within a digital library.

Metadata for Images in XML an XML metadata schema that permits formatting of data assigned to images.

Metadata Object Description Schema an XML schema developed as a bibliographic element set used with MARC 21 records and creating original resource description records.

Metadata Schema metadata elements in which schema identifies content and develops rules for data identifiers for individual elements. The schema is designed in a way so that content can be accessed by multiple users and applications.

METS see Metadata Encoding and Transmission Standard

MIX see Metadata for Images in XML

MODS see Metadata Object Description Schema

Modular Object-Orientated Dynamic Learning Environment an open source learning management system software. Its emphasis is on allowing educators to create online course modules.

Moodle see Modular Object-Orientated Dynamic Learning Environment

MOU see Memorandum of Understanding

Myers-Briggs Type Indicator developed in 1943 by Isabel Briggs Myers, it is an assessment tool listing a total of 16 personality combination types that are designed to indicate psychological likes or preferences in a person's ability of perception and decision making.

Nag Screens windows, screens, or pop-ups that are usually associated with shareware software. Once a version of shareware has been purchased, nag screens will be removed.

N-Factor Authentication see Two-Factor Authentication

No-Problem Syndrome a term that is sometimes used to compensate for a lack of fully understanding all parameters of a particular situation or problem.

OAIS see Open Archival Information System

ONIX see Online Information eXchange

Online Information eXchange an XML schema used in many online book industries for sharing product information about books.

Open Archival Information System an archive that is comprised of both human and computing resources that are committed to preserving information for various communities or organizations.

Open Source Software software that is freely available without costs. Its source code is included along with any needed documentation. Software in this category is often shared, expanded, and built upon networked groups.

Patch a written change source code that is intended to fix potential problems associated with a software program.

PDF see Portable Document Format

PDI see Preservation Description Information

Personal Identifiable User Information a term used to describe information that is personal and allows for systems to identify a particular user.

Petabyte the equivalent to 1,024 terabytes or a million gigabytes.

PHP a scripting language released in 1995. Its use is primarily in creating dynamic web pages.

PmWiki licensed under GNU General Public License, this software allows a user to set up and install a wiki with little computer programming skill.

Portable Document Format a format created by Adobe in 1993, this file format provides a digital image of text and graphics that mirrors the original printed document. This format can then be archived to be transmitted or accessed electronically.

PREMIS see PREservation Metadata Implementation Strategies

Preservation Description Information a term referring to information that is needed to manage content information with which an object is associated.

PREservation Metadata Implementation Strategies an XML metadata schema based on the OAIS model and maintained by the Library of Congress. It consists of a data dictionary that provides information for schema within a repository.

Proprietary Software software developed with legal rights associated with a specific software company. The software is designed in a way that requires a specific interface. The source code is unique to the developer and is often considered the opposite of open source software.

Qualified Dublin Core a continuation of metadata elements from Simple Dublin Core and its original 15 elements.

RDA see Resource Description and Access

Referring URL pertains to the URL of a web page containing the link that was previously used or visited by a user. Referring URLs are often used to predict and analyze the browsing habits of users.

Remix often associated with the term mashup, remix involves taking elements of a program or operation and combining with other programs in order to arrive at a somewhat newer application. It is also referred to in the online music industry as using portions of existing music tracks that have been deconstructed and used for constructing new music tracks.

Repositories see Institutional Repository

Representational State Transfer commonly used for web services, it is a software architecture structure that allows for information to be requested from targeted Web sites for specific data or information.

Resolver sometimes referred to as a link resolver, it is an application that seeks out holding information and access permission to various bibliographic citations. Resolvers can be embedded within various indexing databases to provide links to local holding information or full text access.

Resource Description and Access the new cataloging standard, sometimes referred to as the successor of AACR2. This standard allows for more detailed descriptions assigned to digital objects.

REST see Representational State Transfer

Rich Site Summary also referred to as Really Simple Syndication or RSS, it is a group of XML formats that provides access to web feeds. These feeds give one access to content from a Web site without having to go to or visit a Web site directly. Instead, content is delivered through other means such as an RSS reader program.

RSS see Rich Site Summary

SaaS see Software as a Service

Sakai Project begun in 2004 as an alternative to commercial learning management systems, this open source software learning management system was developed by Stanford, Michigan, Indiana, MIT, and Berkeley.

SDK see Software Development Kit

Secure Sockets Layer Certificate a security-enhanced protocol that is used on web browsers during the exchange of private or personal data. It is versatile and allows for incorporating many encryption schemes.

Semantic Interoperability a term used to describe the ability to interpret information sent by one or more computing systems to a receiving end.

Service Level Agreement a contract of service that is drafted in which level of service is defined or outlined with specific limits.

Service Positioning Markup Language a markup language that is XML based and allows for sharing of user and resource information between cooperating institutions.

Shareware software that is openly distributed with certain restrictions. Once the software is purchased, restrictions or limits are removed and access is allowed to the full version. Shareware often permits usage on a trial by time basis that expires after a certain amount of time, usually after 30 days.

Shibboleth an open source software designed for single sign-on access. This is an example of a federated sign-on software system.

Simple Dublin Core the first level of the Dublin Core schema consisting of 15 elements and used for control of data-field elements within XML.

Single Sign-On a process by which access is granted to multiple points of authentication by one main log-in. This process saves users time by allowing them to log in just once, instead of having to log in at each access point.

SLA see Service Level Agreement

SOAP formally known as Simple Object Access Protocol, it is a protocol for sharing structured information or data between Web sites. It functions by sending/receiving "messages" formatted in XML.

Software as a Service a software distribution and use model that is based on amount of usage or project completion. It is based on the pay-as-you-go model of service.

Software Development Kit a set of software items that includes code sets, documentation, and any other needed software utilities that may be used to develop programs within a specific computer language platform.

SOPAC 2.0 meaning Social OPAC, this Drupal-based content management OPAC system was developed as a way to allow users to interact and add content to existing OPAC records such as reviews, comments, and more. It is open source and data can be shared among multiple library systems.

Source Code text that is developed or drafted by a computer programmer. Source code is interpreted as a set of commands that humans can interact with. The text is then compiled so that a machine or computer can then understand and process an operation.

SPML see Service Positioning Markup Language

SSL Certificate see Secure Sockets Layer Certificate

Structured Data data that is stored or arranged in a way that is fixed within limited fields or arrays. The purpose of such structure exists so that data can be accessed by other programs such as a relational database or spreadsheet program.

Stylesheet a document made up of markup language that describes layout and interaction with other existing documents.

System Level Integration integration that either includes utilities or a certain presence throughout a software system. An example would be the cut, copy, and paste functions of Microsoft Office products; their presence is the same throughout various products.

Tagged Image File Format a format for archiving images and art developed in the mid-1980s. Its primary use is within desktop publishing.

TIFF see Tagged Image File Format

Two-Factor Authentication a process of authentication in which there are two or more points of authentication. In some instances users may be asked for their main password, and then a secondary password must be entered for access.

UNIX an early and somewhat popular operating system. Its code was readily available and was used for developing early Internet programs.

User Identification consists of a string of data that allows a computer system to identify a particular individual apart from other individuals.

Web Proxy sometimes referred to as a proxy server, it is a computer application that allows one or more computers to access computing systems existing on other networks. Its use is primarily to control Web site traffic.

Web Services software components that operate and respond via the Internet. These components allow for large-scale processing such as retail purchases, searching, and delivery of content that performs a function, all from within a particular Web site.

Widget a program or content that is incorporated into an existing Web site. Widgets allow users to perform functions or view information they would normally do from a Web site, from a portal or another existing Web site.

Wiki an online and editable Web site that can be updated or changed by one or more users. They are useful for managing and sharing information that is compiled by a collective of individuals. Wiki is a Hawaiian term meaning quick or speedy, which reflects the process of how content may be updated and presented online.

WordPress an open source, self-hosting blogging tool, which was developed in 2003. It works on a template system, allowing the user to establish a blog without knowing a certain programming code like PHP or HTML.

XML see eXtensible Markup Language

XML Remote Procedure Call similar to SOAP, it operates by sending messages in XML between Web sites and usually sends messages to a targeted server.

XML-RPC see XML Remote Procedure Call

XPath a computing language used for elements with XML documents. It works by selecting units such as character data, data elements, and so forth, and performing either a function or computation with these units.

XSL-FO see Extensible Style Language Formatting Objects

XSLT see Extensible Style Language Transformation

INDEX

ABOUT THE EDITOR
AND CONTRIBUTORS

ELIZABETH L. BLACK is Systems Librarian and Assistant Professor at the Ohio State University Libraries. As Head of the Web Implementation Team, a department within the Libraries' IT Division, she works daily with both librarians and IT professionals. Her responsibilities include the institutional repository, Knowledge Bank; related digital preservation activities; the Libraries' Web site; and the web applications delivered via the Web site. Elizabeth also worked for 13 years at the Columbus Metropolitan Library in a variety of jobs involving technology and customer service. Elizabeth received her Masters of Library Science from Kent State University in Kent, Ohio, and a B.A. and a B.S. from Miami University, Oxford, Ohio.

H. FRANK CERVONE is Vice Chancellor for Information Services at Purdue University Calumet. Previously, he was Assistant University Librarian for Information Technology at Northwestern University in Evanston, Illinois. His research interests include curriculum development and program assessment, human-computer interaction, system and project management methodologies, as well as complex systems and social network analysis in the information professions.

JASON A. CLARK builds digital library applications and sets digital content strategies for Montana State University Libraries. He writes and presents on a broad range of topics ranging from XML and web programming to interface design and metadata. When he's not thinking about APIs, Jason likes to hike the mountains of Montana with his wife, Jennifer; his daughter, Piper;

and his dog, Oakley. You can reach him at jaclark@montana.edu and follow his occasional thoughts about library digital stuff at jasonclark.info or twitter. com/jaclark.

SCOT COLFORD joined the Boston Public Library as Applications Manager in 2003. In 2008 he transitioned to his current position as Web Services Manager. Scot also teaches Technology for Information Professionals at Simmons College Graduate School of Library and Information Science. He blogs at http://libniblets.justgiblets.com and may be reached by email at scolford@bpl.org.

NANCY COURTNEY is Coordinator of Outreach and Engagement at the Ohio State University Libraries and the editor of *Academic Library Outreach: Beyond the Campus Walls* (Libraries Unlimited 2009), *Library 2.0 and Beyond: Innovative Technologies and Tomorrow's User* (Libraries Unlimited, 2007), and *Technology for the Rest of Us: A Primer on Computer Technologies for the Low-Tech Librarian* (Libraries Unlimited, 2005). She has a B.A. in Classics from Northwestern University and an M.S. in Library and Information Science from the University of Illinois.

KIM DUCKETT is Principal Librarian for Digital Technologies and Learning at North Carolina State University where she takes a lead in pushing the library's resources, services, and librarian expertise into online learning environments, especially learning management systems. She is a truly "blended librarian"—equal parts librarian, instructional designer, and learning technologist. She serves as co-project manager and product lead for NCSU Course Views—http://www.lib.ncsu.edu/course—(branded Library Tools), a system that combines dynamically generated and librarian-authored content to create a course-centric set of library resources for more than 6,000 courses. She also identifies the need for and facilitates the creation of "e-learning" projects, including multimedia learning modules and videos. Kim received her M.S.L.S from the University of North Carolina at Chapel Hill in 2001 and was selected as a 2009 *Library Journal* Mover and Shaker.

HECTOR ESCOBAR is a 1999 Spectrum Scholar and a 2000 M.L.I.S. graduate from the University of Texas. A strong advocate for diversity within academic libraries, Hector was selected as University of Notre Dame's first librarian-in-residence. He went on to become the Latino Studies Librarian at Notre Dame. He has served on various committees within the American Library Association (ALA), including being elected to ALA Council. In 2007, Hector became the Director of Education and Information Delivery at the University of Dayton. He currently chairs ALA's Human Resources Development and Recruitment Advisory Committee.

DAVID KENNEDY is an application developer for Duke University Libraries. He previously held positions as application developer for University System of Maryland and Affiliated Institutions (USMAI) and Head of the Office of Digital Collections and Research for University of Maryland. He implemented a single sign-on across library services in the USMAI and was instrumental in the implementation of a single sign-on across the UM campus. David is an active participant in the InCommon Library Services Collaboration.

ARDYS KOZBIAL is the Technology Outreach Librarian in the University of California, San Diego Libraries where much of her current work is focused on digital preservation, especially in collaboration with the San Diego Supercomputer Center (SDSC). Additionally, she works on technology-based grant projects for UCSD, from grant writing to project management, depending on the needs of a particular project. Before coming to UCSD, Ardys spent 12 years working in architecture collections at Harvard University; University of California, Berkeley; the University of Texas at Austin; and Payette Associates (a Boston-based architecture firm) as a librarian and archivist. She received a B.A. from the University of Michigan and an M.S. in Library and Information Science from Simmons College.

STEVE McCANN is the digital projects librarian at the University of Montana Mansfield Library. For the past several years he has been concentrating on digitizing monographs, serials, and photos. He recently served with the writing team that rewrote the BCR (Bibliographical Center for Research) digital imaging best practices document. Prior to entering the library world he worked in the e-commerce industry in Seattle before the Internet bubble burst in 2000. His professional interests revolve around digital preservation, usability, workflow management, and the challenges involved in scaling digitization within small organizations. He also dabbles in cognitive psychology with regard to interface design.

FRANCES RICE is the Director of Information Systems and Digital Access at the Roesch Library at the University of Dayton in Dayton, Ohio. Her main responsibilities are planning, implementing, and maintaining emerging library technologies.

CHRISTOPHER STRAUBER is Humanities Reference Librarian and Coordinator of Instructional Design for Tisch Library at Tufts University. He has worked in web and public services for college and public libraries in South Carolina and Ohio, and with an assortment of corporations.

MAUREEN P. WALSH is an Assistant Professor and Metadata Librarian at the Ohio State University Libraries. As a Metadata Librarian, her work supports the Ohio State University Libraries' digital initiatives, including the Knowledge Bank, the Ohio State University's Institutional Repository. She is also the head of the Libraries' Continuing Resources Cataloging Unit. She is currently serving her second three-year term as a member of OCLC's Collections and Technical Services Advisory Committee. Maureen presents regionally and nationally on metadata and institutional repositories. She has a B.A. in Art History from the University of Cincinnati and an M.L.I.S from Kent State University. Maureen may be contacted by e-mail (walsh.260@osu.edu).